# RUDIMENTS
## OF CHINESE CHARACTER WRITING

# 汉字书写入门

张朋朋 著

北京大学出版社
北 京

**图书在版编目(CIP)数据**

汉字书写入门/张朋朋编著 .-北京:北京大学出版社 1997.12
ISBN 7－307－03330－3
Ⅰ.汉… Ⅱ.张… Ⅲ.汉字-书写规则 Ⅳ.H124.7

书　　　名：汉字书写入门
著作责任者：张朋朋编著
责 任 编 辑：胡双宝
标 准 书 号：ISBN 7-301-03330-3/H·342
出　版　者：北京大学出版社
地　　　址：北京市海淀区中关村北京大学校内　100871
电　　　话：出版部 62752015　发行部 62559712　编辑部 62752032
排　版　者：华伦公司排版部
印　刷　者：北京大学印刷厂
发　行　者：北京大学出版社
经　销　者：新华书店
　　　　　　787×1092毫米　16开本　13印张　330千字
　　　　　　1997年12月第1版　**2002年9月第3次印刷**
定　　　价：28.00元

# 目 录

# CONTENTS

# 导　言

本书是专门为外国人编写的写字课本。

长期以来，汉字被认为是最难学的文字。不少外国学生由于感到汉字难学，从而放弃了继续学习中文的念头。

汉字难学，有它本身复杂的一面，但造成目前汉字如此难学的状况，我认为和我们的教法也有一定的关系。

目前对外国人进行汉字书写教学，基本上采用的是一种"文从语"的教学模式，即汉字教学服从于口语教学，也就是说，学什么话，教什么字。我认为这种教学模式适合拼音文字的教学，而不适合汉字教学。

汉字是形、音、义结合为一体的，每个汉字都有一定的形状，一定的读音，并表示一定的意义。汉字虽然有读音，但它的形体不表示读音，而是表示意义。

汉字是一种表意文字系统。

汉字形体的表意方式是一个富有逻辑性的、有理据的、结构清晰的系统。它最基本的构成要素是笔画。笔画构成独体字，由独体字或由独体字演变而成的偏旁构成合体字。如果在汉字书写教学中，教基本笔画后，先教独体字，再教合体字，按照汉字形体构造的系统性来进行，让学生了解汉字形体的主要表意方式，学会借助意义来记忆字形，这样是会减轻学生学写汉字的难度的。

"文从语"的教学方式使汉字的教学顺序不可能按照汉字形体构造的系统性来进行，必然使汉字的形体书写教学变得杂乱无章。今天教"你好"，明天教"谢谢"，没有充分利用汉字形体的系统性来进行教学，从而增加了教学的难度。

汉语书面语识字教学是可以和写字教学分开的，识字比写字容易得多。字不一定都会写，但可以识读。这是教学中我们看到的事实。既然识字教学可以和写字教学分开，那么，在初学阶段，汉字的书写教学就可以不与书面语识字教学同步，可以独立地进行，可以按照汉字形体构造的特点，先独体字，后合体字，由简单到复杂、由易到难、循序渐进地有规律地进行。对汉字的形体结构进行系统性的教学，不仅可以使写字教学化难为易，而且学生了解了汉字的结构关系对识字教学，即识记字形、字义、字音也会起到促进作用。

常用汉字 3500 多个左右，由于字的构造是有规律的。因此，学生掌握了基本笔画和独体字以及由独体字演变而成的偏旁的写法并了解了汉字的构造规律,他们就具有了分析字形,习得新汉字的能力。所以 3500 个汉字不必个个都教,主要应该让学生了解汉字的构造规律和掌握书写汉字的基本技能。

本着上述精神,我编写了这本写字课本。

本书的编写体例:

第一讲介绍汉字的特点以及汉字和拼音文字的主要区别。

第二讲介绍汉字的基本笔画的写法和笔顺规则。

第三讲介绍独体字在汉字形体构造系统中的基础地位以及独体字中最重要、最常用的 80 来个象形字。对每个象形字都形象地介绍了它们的表意方式(简繁体两种字形)以及字音、字义、笔顺和组词。另外还为学习者提供了练习书写的方格。

第四讲介绍指事字,介绍方式同上。

第五讲介绍 70 来个会意字,这部分增加了合体字组合结构的介绍。

第六讲介绍 80 来个形声字。

第七讲介绍"部首"这一概念并以部首打头,在每一部首下介绍一组具有相同偏旁的汉字。这一讲共介绍 70 来个常用部首和 200 多个汉字。

全书共介绍 400 多个汉字,绝大部分是最常用字,有个别字虽不是最常用字,但也作了介绍,其原因是它们的构字能力强或者是可以作偏旁和部首的字。

为了便于学生查找,书后附有《汉字目录》和《音序检字表》。

本书的编写目的是为了让学生较容易地记忆汉字的字形,培养他们的书写能力,因此,对某些字的分类以及对字的构形关系的分析上由于从教学实用的角度考虑,在处理上与传统或习惯作法不尽相同。这样作可以说是教学上的一种尝试,是否合适也望得到有关专家和同人的批评指正。

张朋朋
1997 年 10 月于北京语言文化大学

# INTRODUCTION

This book is a textbook on how to write Chinese characters prepared specially for foreigners.

For a long time, Chinese characters have been regarded as the most difficult writing, and many foreign students have felt it so hard to learn Chinese characters that they gave up their study of the Chinese language all together.

Chinese characters are hard to learn because they are complex. However, I believe that another reason why the Chinese characters are hard to learn lies in our teaching.

At present, when we teach foreigners Chinese characters, we basically follow the teaching mode of "written after spoken", that is, we teach Chinese characters after we come across them in our talks. I think such teaching mode is suitable for the teaching of the alphabetic system of writing but not for the teaching of Chinese characters.

The form, sound, and meaning of a Chinese character are integrated. Every character has a certain form, pronunciation and meaning. Their forms represent meaning but not pronunciation. Chinese writing is an ideographic system.

Chinese characters have a logical, discernible structure. The basic component is a stroke, of which a number make up an independent character. Independent characters or character components make up combined characters. When we teach written Chinese characters, we teach strokes first, then independent characters, and finally combined characters in order with the structure of the forms of Chinese characters. Students may learn the main meaning of the forms of Chinese characters while memorizing their forms with the help of their meanings. In this way, they will feel it easier to learn and write Chinese characters.

The teaching mode of "written after spoken" does not aidin teaching only throw it into confusion of Chinese characters in their natural order, and will formation. If today you teach "你好" (How are you !), and tomorrow you teach "谢谢" (Thank you.), the writing of these characters cannot be taught in a systematic way, difficulties will be increased.

The teaching of reading Chinese can be separated from that of Chinese character writing. Reading is easier than writing. One who is not able to write down all Chinese characters, may be able to read all of them. This is a fact we have learned from our teaching . Since reading can be separated from writing , the teaching of writing Chinese characters may not go alongside the reading of the written language in the primary stage of learning. It can be carried out independently in accordance with the characteristics of the formation of Chinese characters. By following a natural order and advancing step by step, beginning with independent characters and then combined characters, from the simple to the complex, and from the easy to the difficult. The systematic teaching of the formation of Chinese characters may not only make it easier to teach, but more importantly help students to understand the structural relations between Chinese characters to better remember the form, meaning and pronunciation of a characrter.

There are more than 3500 Chinese characters in common use, each of whose structure has a regular pattern. Therefore, as students master the basic strokes, independent characters and character components, (which were derived from independent characters) as well as the pattern of the structure of the characters, they will be able to analyze the forms of Chinese characters and learn new Chinese characters by themselves. It is not necessary to teach students all the 3500 characters, but it is necessary to help them to understand the pattern of the structure of characters , and master the basic technique of writing them .

It is in the above mentioned spirit, that this textbook is written.

The stylistic rules and layout of the textbook are as follows:

The first chapter introduces the characteristics of Chinese characters, and the major difference between characters and alphabetic writing.

The second chapter introduces the basic strokes for writing Chinese characters and the rules of stroke order observed in calligraphy.

The third chapter introduces the important position of independent Chinese characters in the system of Chinese characters, and the 80 most important and commonly used pictographic characters, each of which has an explanation of its expression (the simplified form and the original complex form) , pronunciation, meaning, strokes and stroke order. There are also places for students to practice writing.

The fourth chapter introduces indicative characters by the above-mentioned method.

The fifth chapter introduces 70 associative characters. It also introduces the structure of combined characters.

The sixth chapter introduces about 80 pictophonograms.

And the seventh chapter introduces the concept of "*Bushou*", radicals by which characters are arranged in Chinese dictionaries, and a group of Chinese characters with the same elements or basic structural parts of Chinese characters under each *Bushou* . This lesson covers 73 *Bushou* in common use and more than 200 characters.

The whole book introduces more than 400 Chinese characters, most of which are characters frequently in use. A few rarely used characters are also introduced. The reason why we introduce them is because of their strong capacity of forming characters and serving as basic structural parts of other Chinese characters or *Bushou* .

To help students to search for Chinese characters, the book has a "Catalogue of Chinese characters" and an "Index of Syllables of the Phonetic Transcriptions of Chinese Characters" attached to it.

The purpose of the book is to help students to easily remember the form of Chinese characters and to acquire the ability to write them. Therefore, the classification of some Chinese characters and the analysis of the structural relations in Chinese characters, which are based on my teaching practice, are different from the convention. This is a first attempt in teaching, and comments from experts and colleagues will be appreciated.

**Zhang Pengpeng**　　August, 1997

# 汉字的特点

## CHARACTERISTICS OF CHINESE CHARACTERS

世界上的文字可分为两大类,一类是表音文字,一类是表意文字。汉字是一种表意文字。

汉字有读音,但汉字的形体不表示读音,而表示意义。也就是说,汉字字形的不同的构造方式表示的是不同的意义。

口          kǒu          mouth

字形          字音          字义

form          pronunciation          meaning

拼音文字字形表音,因此可以借助字音来记忆字形。汉字字形不表音而表意,因此,不可能借助字音来记忆字形结构,那么就要借助字义来记忆字形结构。

汉语识字教学的目的是使字形、字音和字义建立联系,主要是解决汉字的认读问题,而写字教学目的主要是使字义和字形结构建立联系,主要是解决字形书写问题。因此,学习汉字的书写,主要应该了解汉字的形体有哪些表意方式以及是如何以不同的构造方式来表意的,而且要学会通过分析字形来记忆字义,学会借助字义来记忆和书写字形。

The different writing systems of the world can be divided into two categories: phonetic writing systems and semantic writing systems. The Chinese writing system is a semantic one.

Every Chinese character has its pronunciation but its written form does not show it. Instead, it shows the character's semantics. Different forms show different meanings even when the pronunciation is actually the same.

For example.

In alphabetic writing systems, the written form of a word is derived from its pronunciation. We can get help from the pronunciation to memorize the written form. In the Chinese writing system the written form of a character does not give a guide to pronunciation but to meaning. Consequently, one cannot use phonetics to help memorize the written form. It is the meaning of a character that can help in memorizing a character.

The aim in teaching to read is to link up the pronunciation and the written form of a Chinese character in order to be able to read it aloud. The aim in teaching to write is to link up the form of Chinese characters and their meaning in order to express oneself in writing. As a result, in order to learn how to write Chinese characters, one must know the different ways of expressing their meaning as well as their structural form. Through the analysis of Chinese characters one can memorize their meaning. It is also necessary to refer to the meaning of a character to help memorize the written form.

# 2

## 基本笔画和笔顺

## BASIC STROKES AND STROKE ORDER

### 一、基本笔画　Basic strokes

汉字数量虽然很多,但都是由二十几种笔画写成的。拼音文字是字母以线性的方式排列而成的,而汉字是以笔画组合成方块形。汉字笔画有二十多种,在二十几种笔画中最基本的有八种,其余的十几种是在这八种基础上有不同程度的变化。学写汉字首先要掌握基本笔画的写法。对于那些变形笔画将结合具体汉字来学习。

Although there are many Chinese characters, all of them are composed of no more than 30 kinds of strokes. We could draw a parallel to the alphabet which has an inventory of twenty-six letters. The difference is that Chinese is a morpho-syllabic writing while western writing systems are composed of letters. Of the 30 kinds of strokes mentioned above, it is necessary to only learn the eight most important ones and view the others as variants of these.

| | 笔画<br>Strokes | 写法<br>Writing | 要　求<br>Requirement | 例　字<br>Examples | 笔画名称<br>Names |
|---|---|---|---|---|---|
| 1 | 一 | 一 | 从左到右,要平<br>From left to right, level | 二 | 横 héng |
| 2 | 丨 | 丨 | 从上到下,要直<br>From top to bottom, straight | 十 | 竖 shù |
| 3 | 丿 | 丿 | 从上向左下<br>From top to lower left | 八 | 撇 piě |
| 4 | ㇏ | ㇏ | 从左向右下<br>From top to lower right | 大 | 捺 nà |
| 5 | ㇀ | ㇀ | 从下向右上<br>From bottom to upper right | 地 | 提 tí |
| 6 | ㇆ | ㇆ | 先横后竖<br>From left to right and turn down | 口 | 折 zhé |
| 7 | ㇄ | ㇄ | 拐个弯<br>From top to bottom, turn right and<br>tick at the end | 九 | 钩 gōu |
| 8 | 丶 | 丶 | 向右下<br>Dot toward lower right | 六 | 点 diǎn |

**描写基本笔画** Trace the basic strokes

| 1 | 一 | 一 | 一 | 一 | 一 | 一 | 一 | 一 |
|---|---|---|---|---|---|---|---|---|
| | | | | | | | | |
| 2 | 丨 | 丨 | 丨 | 丨 | 丨 | 丨 | 丨 | 丨 |
| | | | | | | | | |
| 3 | 丿 | 丿 | 丿 | 丿 | 丿 | 丿 | 丿 | 丿 |
| | | | | | | | | |
| 4 | 乀 | 乀 | 乀 | 乀 | 乀 | 乀 | 乀 | 乀 |
| | | | | | | | | |
| 5 | 丶 | 丶 | 丶 | 丶 | 丶 | 丶 | 丶 | 丶 |
| | | | | | | | | |
| 6 | 乛 | 乛 | 乛 | 乛 | 乛 | 乛 | 乛 | 乛 |
| | | | | | | | | |
| 7 | 乚 | 乚 | 乚 | 乚 | 乚 | 乚 | 乚 | 乚 |
| | | | | | | | | |
| 8 | 丶 | 丶 | 丶 | 丶 | 丶 | 丶 | 丶 | 丶 |
| | | | | | | | | |

## 二、笔顺规则　Rules of stroke order

组成一个汉字的笔画在书写时是有一定顺序的。也就是说,有的笔画要先写,有的笔画要后写。按照正确的笔顺规则书写汉字,可以提高书写的速度和字形的准确性。

笔顺规则是指在书写独体字时哪一笔先写,哪一笔后写的问题。书写合体字有一个结构顺序问题,也就是哪一部分先写,哪一部分后写。

本讲只介绍笔顺规则。有关合体字的结构顺序,将在第五讲"合体字的结构"中介绍。

In writing Chinese characters, one should follow a certain order of the strokes which compose a character, some strokes proceed others. Following the correct stroke-order one can raise the speed of writing and ensure correctness.

Stroke-order is especially important for writing independent characters. In writing combined characters, one should follow the order of structure, some components proceed others.

This chapter presents the rules of stroke-order. About the structural rules in combined characters, see Chapter 5 "Structure of the combined character".

| | 规　则<br>Rules | 例　字<br>Examples | 笔　顺<br>Stroke-order |
|---|---|---|---|
| 1 | 先横后竖<br>"heng" before "shu" | 十 | 一 十 |
| 2 | 先撇后捺<br>"pie" before "na" | 人 | 丿 人 |
| 3 | 先上后下<br>From top to bottom | 二 | 一 二 |
| 4 | 先左后右<br>From left to right | 儿 | 丿 儿 |
| 5 | 先中间后两边<br>Middle before the two sides | 小 | 亅 小 小 |
| 6 | 先外后内<br>From outside to inside | 月 | 丿 刀 月 月 |
| 7 | 先进后封口<br>Inside before the sealing stroke | 回 | 丨 冂 冋 回 回 |

# 3

## 独体字(上)－象形字

## INDEPENDENT CHARACTERS(1) — PICTOGRAMS

### 独体字和合体字

汉字从形体构造上可分为两大类。一类是独体字,一类是合体字。独体字是指由笔画组成的、不能再分成两部分的字。合体字是指由两个或两个以上部分组成的字。

从构造上来分析,构成合体字的部分,有的就是一个独体字,或者是由独体字演变而来的符号。因此,独体字是学习汉字的基础。掌握了独体字,理解和书写合体字就容易了。

### 象形字

独体字从表意方式上分为两种,一种是象形字,一种是指事字。字的形状像所表示的具体事物,这种字叫象形字。

象形字占常用汉字总数的 5 %左右。虽然它的数量少,但它是学习汉字形体构造系统的最重要的一部分。

### Independent characters and combined characters

Chinese characters can be divided into two categories : independent characters and combined characters. Independent characters consist of elementary strokes which cannot be subdivided.

With regard to structure, independent characters are the basic elements out of which combined characters are made up. Combined characters will be easier to understand and write once independent characters have been mastered.

### Pictograms

From the way they express meaning, independent characters can again be subdivided into two kinds: pictograms and indicative characters. Pictograms represent in stylized form the objects they refer to.

although only 5 % of all Chinese characters belong to the pictographic kind, but they are of crucial importance to the mastery of the structure of Chinese characters.

rén　human being

| 人民 | rénmín | people |
|---|---|---|
| 人口 | rénkǒu | population |
| 大人 | dàrén | adult |

 →  →  →

古代"人"的写法像一个侧立的人形。
The ancient form of "人" shows a standing man in profile.

| 丿 | 人 |  |  |  |  |  |  |  |  |
|---|---|---|---|---|---|---|---|---|---|
| 人 |  |  |  |  |  |  |  |  |  |

 dà　big, great

| 大家 | dàjiā | everybody |
|---|---|---|
| 大学 | dàxué | university |
| 大人 | dàrén | adult |

 →  →  →  →

古代"大"字像一个正面站立两臂张开,高大的人形。
The ancient form of "大" shows the frontal view of a tall man standing with arms and legs spread out.

| 一 | 𠂇 | 大 |  |  |  |  |  |  |  |
|---|---|---|---|---|---|---|---|---|---|
| 大 |  |  |  |  |  |  |  |  |  |

6

# 夫 fū husband, man

丈夫 zhàngfu husband
大夫 dàifu doctor
夫人 fūren wife

古代"夫"字像一个正面直立的人形,上面的一横表示头发上插一根簪,意指已成年的男子。

The ancient form of "夫" shows the frontal view of a man with a pin through his hair, which signifies that he has reached adulthood.

| 一 | 二 | 夫 | 夫 | | | | | | |
|---|---|---|---|---|---|---|---|---|---|
| 夫 | | | | | | | | | |

# 立 lì stand, set up

站立 zhànlì stand
立刻 lìkè at once
成立 chénglì found

古代"立"字像一人两腿分开,在地上站立着。

The ancient form of "立" shows a man standing on the ground with his legs apart.

| 丶 | 二 | 六 | 立 | 立 | | | | | |
|---|---|---|---|---|---|---|---|---|---|
| 立 | | | | | | | | | |

# 刀　　dāo　　knife

| 刀子 | dāozi | pocketknife |
| 剪刀 | jiǎndāo | scissors |
| 开刀 | kāidāo | operate |

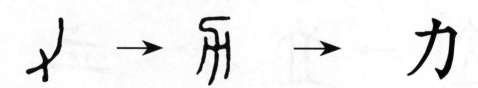

古代"刀"的写法像一把刀子的形状,上面是刀把,下面是刀身。

The ancient form of "刀" looks like a knife, the upper part standing for the handle, and the lower part the blade.

| 刁 | 刀 |  |  |  |  |  |  |  |
|---|---|---|---|---|---|---|---|---|

| 刀 |  |  |  |  |  |  |  |  |
|---|---|---|---|---|---|---|---|---|

# 力　　lì　　force, power

| 力量 | lì liang | force |
| 努力 | nǔlì | work hard |
| 权力 | quánlì | power |

古代"力"字像古代的一种翻土的农具,种地需要用力,所以用它表示力气和力量。

The ancient form of "力" looks like a garden tool; to turn up soil one needs strength, therefore this character means strength or power.

| 丁 | 力 |  |  |  |  |  |  |  |
|---|---|---|---|---|---|---|---|---|

| 力 |  |  |  |  |  |  |  |  |
|---|---|---|---|---|---|---|---|---|

# 儿 [兒]　　ér　　child, son

儿子　érzi　son
女儿　nǚér　daughter
儿童　értóng　children

古代"儿"字像一个大头的小孩儿形状,繁体字"兒"还保留一点这样的意思。
The ancient form of "儿" looks like a child with a big head.

| 丿 | 儿 |  |  |  |  |  |  |  |  |  |
|---|---|---|---|---|---|---|---|---|---|---|
| 儿 |  |  |  |  |  |  |  |  |  |  |

# 子　　zǐ　　son, child

孩子　háizi　child
子女　zǐnǚ　children
女子　nǚzǐ　woman

古代"子"像一个在襁褓中两臂张开的婴儿。
The ancient form of "子" shows a baby in his swaddling clothes with his arms raised.

| ㄱ | 了 | 子 |  |  |  |  |  |  |  |  |
|---|---|---|---|---|---|---|---|---|---|---|
| 子 |  |  |  |  |  |  |  |  |  |  |

# 口      kǒu      mouth

口才    kǒucái    eloquence
门口    ménkǒu    entrance
路口    lùkǒu    crossing

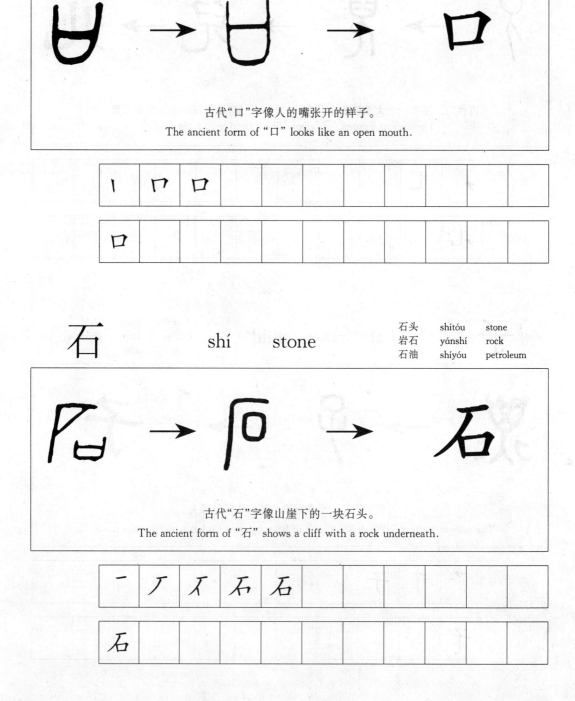

古代"口"字像人的嘴张开的样子。
The ancient form of "口" looks like an open mouth.

| 丨 | 冂 | 口 | | | | | | | |
|---|---|---|---|---|---|---|---|---|---|
| 口 | | | | | | | | | |

# 石      shí      stone

石头    shítóu    stone
岩石    yánshí    rock
石油    shíyóu    petroleum

古代"石"字像山崖下的一块石头。
The ancient form of "石" shows a cliff with a rock underneath.

| 一 | 丆 | 尤 | 石 | 石 | | | | | |
|---|---|---|---|---|---|---|---|---|---|
| 石 | | | | | | | | | |

# 厂 [廠]　chǎng　factory, yard

工厂　gōngchǎng　factory
厂房　chǎngfáng　workshop
厂长　chǎngzhǎng　factory director

古代"厂"字像山崖的形状。现在用作"厂"的简化字。

The ancient form of "厂" resembles a cliff. Today it is used as a simplified form of "廠"(factory).

| 一 | 厂 |  |  |  |  |  |  |  |  |
|---|---|---|---|---|---|---|---|---|---|
| 厂 |  |  |  |  |  |  |  |  |  |

# 广 [廣]　guǎng　wide, vast

广大　guǎngdà　vast
广泛　guǎngfàn　extensive
推广　tuīguǎng　popularize

古代"广"字像靠山崖建造的有屋顶的房屋。今用作"广"的简化字。

The ancient form of "广" looks like a house with a roof by the side of a cilff. Today it is the simplified form of "廣".

| 、 | 亠 | 广 |  |  |  |  |  |  |  |
|---|---|---|---|---|---|---|---|---|---|
| 广 |  |  |  |  |  |  |  |  |  |

11

日　　rì　　sun, day

| 日子 | rìzi | day |
| 日期 | rìqī | date |
| 日本 | Rìběn | Japan |

古代"日"的写法像天上的太阳。
The ancient form of "日" resembles the sun.

| l | 冂 | 日 | 日 | | | | | | |
|---|---|---|---|---|---|---|---|---|---|

| 日 | | | | | | | | | |
|---|---|---|---|---|---|---|---|---|---|

白　　bái　　white, clear

| 白色 | báisè | white |
| 白天 | báitiān | daytime |
| 明白 | míngbai | clear |

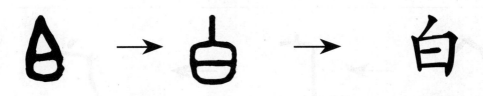

古代"白"字像日始出地面向上闪耀着微光。
The ancient form of "白" shows a flash of light emitting from the rising sun.

| ' | 亻 | 白 | 白 | 白 | | | | | |
|---|---|---|---|---|---|---|---|---|---|

| 白 | | | | | | | | | |
|---|---|---|---|---|---|---|---|---|---|

月　　yuè　moon, month

| 月亮 | yuèliang | the moon |
| 月底 | yuèdǐ | the end of a month |
| 月初 | yuèchū | early in a month |

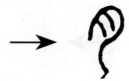

古代"月"字像晚上天空中的一轮弯月。
The ancient form of "月" looks like a crescent at night.

| 丿 | 刀 | 月 | 月 | | | | | | |

| 月 | | | | | | | | | |

井　　jǐng　well

| 井口 | jǐngkǒu | the mouth of a well |
| 水井 | shuǐjǐng | well |
| 矿井 | kuàngjǐng | pit |

井 → 井 → 井

古代"井"字像四边有栏杆的井口形。
The ancient form of "井" shows the mouth of a well with railings on the four sides.

| 一 | 二 | 尹 | 井 | | | | | | |

| 井 | | | | | | | | | |

13

小　　xiǎo　small, little

| 小学 | xiǎoxué | primary school |
| 小说 | xiǎoshuō | novel |
| 小心 | xiǎoxīn | take care |

古代"小"字像几颗微小的沙粒,以表示物体很小。
The ancient form of "小" shows several grains of sand to indicate the smallness of a thing.

| 亅 | 小 | 小 | | | | | |
|---|---|---|---|---|---|---|---|
| 小 | | | | | | | |

水　　shuǐ　water

| 水果 | shuǐguǒ | fruit |
| 汽水 | qìshuǐ | soda water |
| 水平 | shuǐpíng | level |

 →  → 水

古代"水"的写法像水流动的样子,水流旁边是溅起的水花。
The ancient form of "水" is written as running water with spray on the two sides.

| 亅 | 小 | 水 | 水 | | | | |
|---|---|---|---|---|---|---|---|
| 水 | | | | | | | |

门 [門]     **mén**    door, gate

| 大门 | dàmén | gate |
|------|-------|------|
| 门票 | ménpiào | entrance ticket |
| 车门 | chēmén | automobile door |

古代"門"字像两扇门,简化后的"门"字仍可看出门的轮廓。

The ancient form of "門" shows two door leaves, the simplified pictogram "门" still retains the shape of a door.

| 丶 | 𠃋 | 门 | | | | | | |
|---|---|---|---|---|---|---|---|---|

| 门 | | | | | | | | |
|---|---|---|---|---|---|---|---|---|

户     **hù**     door, household

| 户口 | hùkǒu | registered residence |
|------|-------|------|
| 窗户 | chuānghu | window |
| 住户 | zhùhù | household |

古代"户"字像"门"字的一半。

The ancient form of "户" shows a single-leaf door and looks like one half of the character "门" above.

| 丶 | ⸜ | 彐 | 户 | | | | | |
|---|---|---|---|---|---|---|---|---|

| 户 | | | | | | | | |
|---|---|---|---|---|---|---|---|---|

15

# 工　gōng　work, labour

| | | |
|---|---|---|
| 工人 | gōngrén | worker |
| 工作 | gōngzuò | work, job |
| 工厂 | gōngchǎng | factory |

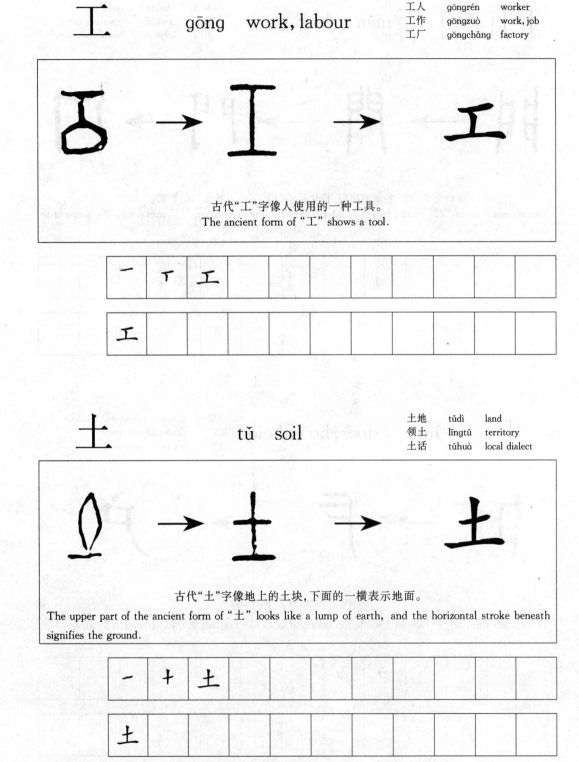

古代"工"字像人使用的一种工具。
The ancient form of "工" shows a tool.

# 土　tǔ　soil

| | | |
|---|---|---|
| 土地 | tǔdì | land |
| 领土 | lǐngtǔ | territory |
| 土话 | tǔhuà | local dialect |

古代"土"字像地上的土块,下面的一横表示地面。
The upper part of the ancient form of "土" looks like a lump of earth, and the horizontal stroke beneath signifies the ground.

**shān** hill, mountain

山口　shānkǒu　mountain pass
大山　dàshān　big hill
山水　shānshuǐ　landscape

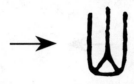 →

古代"山"字像三个并排、重叠的山峰。
The ancient form of "山" shows three peaks next to each other.

| 丨 | 凵 | 山 | | | | | | | |
|---|---|---|---|---|---|---|---|---|---|

| 山 | | | | | | | | | |
|---|---|---|---|---|---|---|---|---|---|

 **jīn** towel, kerchief

手巾　shǒujīn　towel
毛巾　máojīn　towel
头巾　tóujīn　scarf

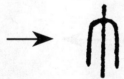 →  →

古代"巾"字像挂着的一条手巾或围巾。
The ancient form of "巾" shows a scarf or a towel hanging down.

| 丨 | 冂 | 巾 | | | | | | | |
|---|---|---|---|---|---|---|---|---|---|

| 巾 | | | | | | | | | |
|---|---|---|---|---|---|---|---|---|---|

木　　　mù　tree, wood

| 木头 | mùtou | wood |
| 树木 | shùmù | tree |
| 木材 | mùcái | wood |

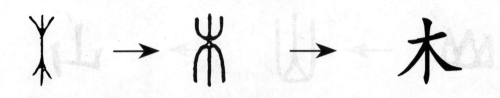

古代"木"字像一棵树,向上的部分表示树枝,向下的部分表示树根。
The ancient form of "木" resembles a tree. Its upper part signals the branches, the lower part the root.

| 一 | 十 | 才 | 木 | | | | | | |
| 木 | | | | | | | | | |

果　　　guǒ　fruit

| 水果 | shuǐguǒ | fruit |
| 果树 | guǒshù | fruit tree |
| 结果 | jiéguǒ | result |

古代"果"字像一棵树上结了果实。
The ancient form of "果" shows a tree bearing fruit.

| 丶 | 冂 | 冋 | 日 | 旦 | 甲 | 臾 | 果 | | |
| 果 | | | | | | | | | |

**hé standing grain**

禾苗 　 hémiáo 　 seedlings of grain
禾本科植物 　 　 plants of the grass family
héběnkē zhíwù

古代"禾"字像一株穗实饱满的谷子,沉甸甸的谷穗向下低垂着。
The ancient form of "禾" shows a plump-eared millet with the stalk bending under its own weight.

| 一 | 二 | 千 | 禾 | 禾 | | | | | |
|---|---|---|---|---|---|---|---|---|---|

| 禾 | | | | | | | | | |
|---|---|---|---|---|---|---|---|---|---|

 **mǐ rice**

大米 　 dàmǐ 　 rice
米饭 　 mǐfàn 　 (cooked) rice
小米 　 xiǎomǐ 　 millet

 →  →

古代"米"字像许多颗米粒。
The ancient form of "米" shows several grains of rice.

| 、 | 、、 | 丷 | 半 | 米 | 米 | | | | |
|---|---|---|---|---|---|---|---|---|---|

| 米 | | | | | | | | | |
|---|---|---|---|---|---|---|---|---|---|

女     nǚ     woman

| 女人 | nǚrén | woman |
| 女儿 | nǚ'ér | daughter |
| 女孩 | nǚhái | girl |

古代"女"字像一两手交叉于前,屈膝跪坐的妇女形。
The ancient form of "女" shows a woman kneeling down with her hands crossed in the front.

| 〈 | 女 | 女 | | | | | | | |
|---|---|---|---|---|---|---|---|---|---|

| 女 | | | | | | | | | |
|---|---|---|---|---|---|---|---|---|---|

母     mǔ     mother

| 母亲 | mǔqīn | mothr |
| 父母 | fùmǔ | father and mother |
| 母马 | mǔmǎ | mare |

古代"母"字像胸前有一对乳房的跪坐着的妇人。
The ancient form of "母" shows a kneeling woman with her two breasts clearly indicated.

| ㄥ | 毋 | 母 | 母 | 母 | | | | | |
|---|---|---|---|---|---|---|---|---|---|

| 母 | | | | | | | | | |
|---|---|---|---|---|---|---|---|---|---|

丁　　　dīng　cubes, man

| 肉丁 | ròudīng | diced meat |
| 园丁 | yuándīng | gardener |
| 人丁 | réndīng | population |

↑ → 个 → 丁

古代"丁"字像一颗钉子的形状。
The ancient form of "丁" looks like a nail.

| 一 | 丁 | | | | | | | |
|---|---|---|---|---|---|---|---|---|

| 丁 | | | | | | | | |
|---|---|---|---|---|---|---|---|---|

示　　　shì　show, notify

| 表示 | biǎoshì | show |
| 指示 | zhǐshì | indicate |
| 告示 | gàoshi | notice |

示 → 示 → 示

古代"示"字像祭祀鬼神的供桌。
The ancient form of "示" shows an altar to offer sacrifices to spirits and gods.

| 一 | 二 | 亍 | 示 | 示 | | | | |
|---|---|---|---|---|---|---|---|---|

| 示 | | | | | | | | |
|---|---|---|---|---|---|---|---|---|

# 又     yòu    again, and

又及    yòují    postscript
又…又        both…and…
yòu…yòu…

古代"又"字像右手张开、向上。
The ancient form of "又" shows an open right hand.

| 丁 | 又 | | | | | | | |
|---|---|---|---|---|---|---|---|---|
| 又 | | | | | | | | |

# 尸     shī    corpse

尸体    shītǐ    corpse
死尸    sǐshī    dead body
尸骨    shīgǔ    skeleton

古代"尸"字像人体挺直、端坐的样子。
The ancient form of "尸" shows a body sitting up very straight. the body of a dead man lying on his side.

| ㄱ | ㄱ | 尸 | | | | | | | |
|---|---|---|---|---|---|---|---|---|---|
| 尸 | | | | | | | | | |

爪　　zhuǎ　claw, talon

爪子　zhuǎzi　claw
爪儿　zhuǎr　paw
猫爪　māozhuǎ　a cat's paws

 →  →

　　古代"爪"字像手指张开抓物之形。后来专指动物的鸟兽的爪。

The ancient form of "爪" shows a hand with its fingers stretching out for something. Now this character is used to specially refer to the claw of birds and other animals.

| ´ | 厂 | 爪 | 爪 | | | | | | |
|---|---|---|---|---|---|---|---|---|---|
| 爪 | | | | | | | | | |

斤　　jīn　（a unit of weight）

一斤　yījīn　0.5kilogram
公斤　gōngjīn　kilogram
斤两　jīnliǎng　weight

 →  → 斤

　　古代"斤"字像有锋刃的斧子。

The ancient form of "斤" shows an axe with a sharp edge.

| ´ | 厂 | 斤 | 斤 | | | | | | |
|---|---|---|---|---|---|---|---|---|---|
| 斤 | | | | | | | | | |

王　　　**wáng　king**

| 国王 | guówáng | king |
| 王子 | wángzǐ | prince |
| 王后 | wánghòu | queen |

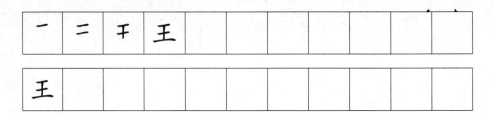

古代"王"字像一人上顶天、下踩地、肃容而立。
The ancient form of "王" shows a man standing seriously on the ground with his head touching the sky.

| 一 | 二 | 王 | 王 | | | | | | |
|---|---|---|---|---|---|---|---|---|---|

| 王 | | | | | | | | | |
|---|---|---|---|---|---|---|---|---|---|

玉　　　**yù　jade**

| 玉石 | yùshí | jade |
| 玉器 | yùqì | jade article |
| 玉米 | yùmǐ | maize |

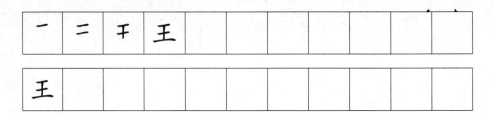

古代"玉"字像一根绳子串着一些片状的玉石。
The ancient form of "玉" resembls some slices of jade strung together with a cord.

| 一 | 二 | 王 | 王 | 玉 | | | | | |
|---|---|---|---|---|---|---|---|---|---|

| 玉 | | | | | | | | | |
|---|---|---|---|---|---|---|---|---|---|

**shǒu hand**

手续 shǒuxù formalities
手巾 shǒujīn towel
手套 shǒutào gloves

 →  →

古代"手"字像一只手张开的样子,后来的写法就看不出手指的形状了。

The ancient form of "手" looks like an open hand; with the evolution of its form, it is no longer pictarclike now.

| 一 | 二 | 三 | 手 | | | | | | |
|---|---|---|---|---|---|---|---|---|---|
| 手 | | | | | | | | | |

 **máo hair, wool**

毛衣 máoyī sweater
毛笔 máobǐ writing brush
毛巾 máojīn towel

 →  →

古代"毛"字像人或动物身上长出的一根根毛发。

The ancient form of "毛" shows the hairs of a person or animal.

| 一 | 二 | 三 | 毛 | | | | | | |
|---|---|---|---|---|---|---|---|---|---|
| 毛 | | | | | | | | | |

25

牛　　　　　niú　ox

牛奶　niúnǎi　milk
牛肉　niúròu　beef
奶牛　nǎiniú　milch cow

古代"牛"字像从正面看的牛头，上边是高高翘起的牛角，中间一竖表示牛面，下边一横表示牛耳。
The ancient form of "牛" shows the head of an ox; the curves on the two sides standing for the horns, the vertical stroke the face, and the lower horizontal stroke the ears.

| ⸌ | ⸌ | 二 | 牛 | | | | | | | |

| 牛 | | | | | | | | | | |

羊　　　　　yáng　sheep

羊毛　yángmáo　sheep's wool
羊肉　yángròu　mutton
母羊　mǔyáng　ewe

古代"羊"字像从正面看的羊头，两只向下弯曲的羊角和尖尖的下巴。
The ancient form of "羊" shows the frontal view of a sheep's head with its two curved horns and pointed chin.

| 丶 | 丷 | 䒑 | 兰 | 兰 | 羊 | | | | |

| 羊 | | | | | | | | | |

26

**fù father**

父亲　fùqin　father
父母　fùmǔ　parents
父子　fùzǐ　father and son

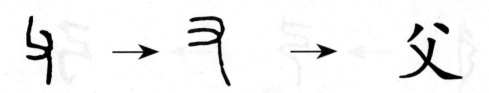

古代"父"字像手持棍棒在教训子女。

The ancient form of "父" consists of a hand part and a stroke standing for a stick, referring to someone with the right to punish a child, i. e. father.

| ′ | ハ | ゲ | 父 | | | | | | |
|---|---|---|---|---|---|---|---|---|---|

| 父 | | | | | | | | | |
|---|---|---|---|---|---|---|---|---|---|

 **wén script, writing**

中文　zhōngwén　Chinese
文化　wénhuà　culture
文学　wénxué　literature

 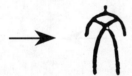  

古代"文"字像一个人身上刺有交错花纹。

The ancient form of "文" shows a man with criss-cross lines i. e. tattoos, on his chest.

| 、 | 一 | ナ | 文 | | | | | | |
|---|---|---|---|---|---|---|---|---|---|

| 文 | | | | | | | | | |
|---|---|---|---|---|---|---|---|---|---|

弓      gōng    bow

| 弓子 | gōngzi | bow(an instrument) |
| 弓箭 | gōngjiàn | bow and arrow |
| 弓形 | gōngxíng | bow-shaped |

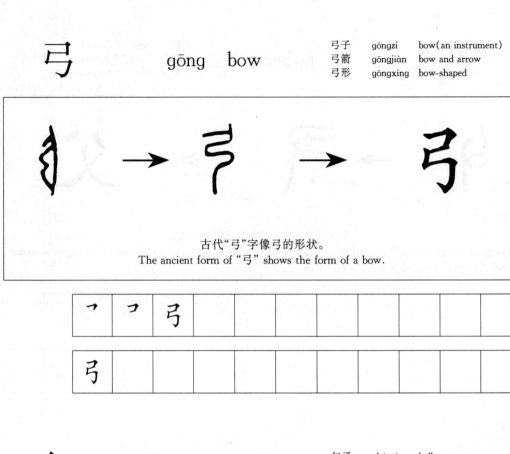

古代"弓"字像弓的形状。
The ancient form of "弓" shows the form of a bow.

勺      sháo    spoon, ladle

| 勺子 | sháozi | ladle |
| 小勺 | xiǎosháo | spoon |
| 汤勺 | tāngsháo | soup ladle |

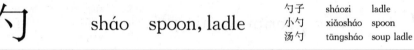

古代"勺"字像一种舀酒的器皿。
The ancient form of "勺" shows a spoon-like utensil for lifting wine.

**xīn  heart**

心脏    xīnzàng    the heart
关心    guānxīn    care for
放心    fàngxīn    be at ease

 →  →

古代"心"字像一个心脏的外形。
The ancient form of "心" looks like the form of a heart.

| 丶 | 心 | 心 | 心 | | | | | | |
|---|---|---|---|---|---|---|---|---|---|

| 心 | | | | | | | | | |
|---|---|---|---|---|---|---|---|---|---|

 **huǒ  fire**

火柴    huǒchái    match
火车    huǒchē    train
火山    huǒshān    volcano

 →  →

古代"火"字像火焰的形状。
The ancient form of "火" shows the flames of a burning substance.

| 丶 | 丷 | 少 | 火 | | | | | | |
|---|---|---|---|---|---|---|---|---|---|

| 火 | | | | | | | | | |
|---|---|---|---|---|---|---|---|---|---|

# 车 [車]　　　chē　　vehicle

汽车　qìchē　motor vehicle
火车　huǒchē　train
马车　mǎchē　carriage

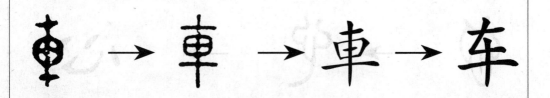

古代"车"的写法中间像车箱,上下两横像俯视的两个车轮,中间的一竖是车轴。
The ancient form of "车" shows a chariot seen from above: the central rectangular standing for the carriage, the vertical stroke the axle and the horizontal strokes on the two sides the wheels.

| 一 | 𠃊 | 𢎥 | 车 | | | | | |
|---|---|---|---|---|---|---|---|---|
| 车 | | | | | | | | |

# 虫 [蟲]　　　chóng　　insect

虫子　chóngzi　insect;worm
昆虫　kūnchóng　insect
害虫　hàichóng　injurious insect

古代"虫"字像一条虫子的样子,有头,有尾和弯曲的虫身。
The ancient form of "虫" shows the shape of a worm, especially its pointed head and beut tail.

| 丶 | 丷 | 口 | 口 | 中 | 虫 | 虫 | | |
|---|---|---|---|---|---|---|---|---|
| 虫 | | | | | | | | |

# 马 [馬]　　　mǎ　horse

马力　mǎlì　horsepower
马车　mǎchē　carriage
马上　mǎshàng　at once

𦮠 → 馬 → 馬 → 马

古代"马"字像一匹马的样子,有长长的鬃毛和马尾以及可以奔跑的四条腿。
The ancient form of "马" looks like a horse, with its mane, legs and tail.

| フ | 马 | 马 | | | | | | | |
|---|---|---|---|---|---|---|---|---|---|
| 马 | | | | | | | | | |

# 鸟 [鳥]　　　niǎo　bird

小鸟　xiǎoniǎo　little bird
鸟类　niǎolèi　birds
候鸟　hòuniǎo　migrant

𠽤 → 鳥 → 鳥 → 鸟

古代"鸟"字像一只鸟的样子,有鸟头、鸟爪和翅膀。
The ancient form of "鸟" shows a bird with its head, talons and wings.

| ′ | ⺈ | 勹 | 鸟 | 鸟 | | | | | |
|---|---|---|---|---|---|---|---|---|---|
| 鸟 | | | | | | | | | |

飞 [飛]      fēi    plane

| 飞机 | fēijī | plane |
| 起飞 | qǐfēi | take off |
| 飞快 | fēikuài | very fast |

飛 → 飛 → 飞

古代"飞"字像一只鸟展翅飞翔的样子。
The ancient form of "飞" shows a bird in flight with its wings spread.

| 乁 | 飞 | 飞 | | | | | | | |
| 飞 | | | | | | | | | |

气 [氣]      qì    air, gas

| 天气 | tiānqì | weather |
| 空气 | kōngqì | air |
| 气体 | qìtǐ | gas |

气 → 氣 → 氣 → 气

古代"气"字像气体升腾的样子。
The ancient form of "气" looks like the way gas rises up.

| ノ | 乁 | 气 | 气 | | | | | | |
| 气 | | | | | | | | | |

32

# 贝 [貝]　　bèi　shellfish

宝贝　bǎobèi　treasure
贝壳　bèiké　shell
贝雕　bèidiāo　shell carving

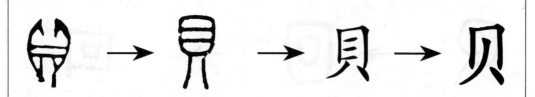

古代"贝"字像一个打开的贝壳的形状。贝壳是珍贵的饰物,曾用作货币。

The ancient form of "贝" shows the ventral view of a shell; in the early stages of civilization shells were used as money, thus this pictogram may refer to a treasure of something valuable.

| 丨 | 冂 | 𠈑 | 贝 |  |  |  |  |  |  |
|---|---|---|---|---|---|---|---|---|---|

| 贝 |  |  |  |  |  |  |  |  |  |
|---|---|---|---|---|---|---|---|---|---|


# 页 [頁]　　yè　　page

一页　yīyè　one page
页码　yèmǎ　page number
活页　huóyè　loose leaf

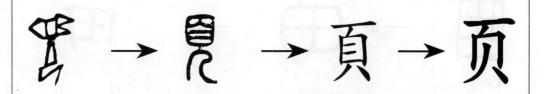

"页"的本义指"头"。古代"页"字上部是一个大大的人头,下部的身体很小。

The original meaning of "页" is head. Its ancient form looks like a big head on top of a small body.

| 一 | 丆 | 厂 | 页 | 页 | 页 |  |  |  |  |
|---|---|---|---|---|---|---|---|---|---|

| 页 |  |  |  |  |  |  |  |  |  |
|---|---|---|---|---|---|---|---|---|---|

回　　huí　circle, return

回去　huíqù　go back
回家　huíjiā　go home
回答　huídá　answer

古代"回"字像水流回旋的样子。
The ancient form of "回" shows circular currents of water, i.e. a whirlpool.

| 丨 | 冂 | 冂 | 冋 | 回 | 回 | | | | | | |

| 回 | | | | | | | | | | | |

田　　tián　field, farmland

田地　tiándì　field
田径　tiánjìng　track and field
油田　yóutián　oilfield

古代"田"字像一块块田地，田埂纵横交错。
The ancient form of "田" shows a piece of cultivated land and paths for peasants to walk on.

| 丨 | 冂 | 冃 | 甲 | 田 | | | | | | | |

| 田 | | | | | | | | | | | |

34

# 鱼 [魚]　　yú　　fish

| | | |
|---|---|---|
| 鱼肉 | yúròu | the flesh of fish |
| 鱼子 | yúzǐ | roe |
| 钓鱼 | diàoyú | to fish |

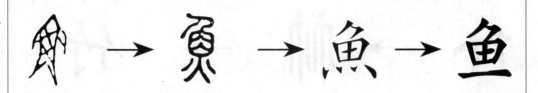

古代"鱼"字像一条鱼的样子,可以看出鱼头、鱼身、鱼鳞和鱼鳍。
The ancient form of "鱼" shows a fish with its head, body, scales, and fins.

| ⺈ | ⺈ | ⺈ | 刍 | 刍 | 鱼 | 鱼 | 鱼 | | | |
|---|---|---|---|---|---|---|---|---|---|---|
| 鱼 | | | | | | | | | | |

# 长 [長]　　cháng　　long

| | | |
|---|---|---|
| 长城 | chángchéng | the Great Wall |
| 长江 | chángjiāng | the Yangtze River |
| 长短 | chángduǎn | length |

古代"长"字像一个人披着很长的头发。
The ancient form of "长" shows a person with long hair.

| ⺈ | 二 | 七 | 长 | | | | | | | |
|---|---|---|---|---|---|---|---|---|---|---|
| 长 | | | | | | | | | | |

# 竹　　zhú　bamboo

| 竹子 | zhúzi | bamboo |
| 竹叶 | zhúyè | bamboo leaf |
| 文竹 | wénzhú | asparagus fern |

古代"竹"字像竹叶的形状。
The ancient form of "竹" shows the shape of bamboo leaves.

| ノ | ᰋ | 彳 | 竹 | 竹 | 竹 | | | | |
|---|---|---|---|---|---|---|---|---|---|

| 竹 | | | | | | | | | |
|---|---|---|---|---|---|---|---|---|---|

# 行　　háng　line, row, trade

| 行列 | hángliè | ranks |
| 行业 | hángyè | trade |
| 银行 | yínháng | band |

古代"行"字像一个十字路口。
The ancient form of "行" resembles a crossroads .

| ノ | ⼃ | 彳 | 彳 | 行 | 行 | | | | |
|---|---|---|---|---|---|---|---|---|---|

| 行 | | | | | | | | | |
|---|---|---|---|---|---|---|---|---|---|

目     mù   eye

| 目的 | mùdì | purpose |
| 目前 | mùqián | at present |
| 节目 | jiémù | programme |

古代"目"字像人的一只眼睛，后来竖起来写，就成了现在的"目"字。
The ancient form of "目" first shows a horizontal eye; but it has evolved into its present vertical form now.

| 丨 | 冂 | 冃 | 月 | 目 | | | | | |
|---|---|---|---|---|---|---|---|---|---|

| 目 | | | | | | | | | |
|---|---|---|---|---|---|---|---|---|---|

首     shǒu   head, first

| 首都 | shǒudū | capital |
| 首先 | shǒuxiān | first |
| 首次 | shǒucì | for the first time |

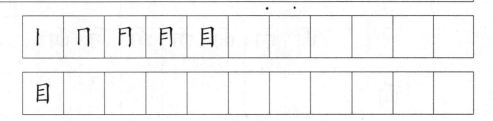

古代"首"字像一人头，上边是头盖和毛发，下边是眼睛。
The ancient form of "首" shows a person's head, the upper part showing the hair on the head, the lower part his eyes.

| 丶 | 丷 | 丷 | 䒑 | 产 | 产 | 首 | 首 | 首 | |
|---|---|---|---|---|---|---|---|---|---|

| 首 | | | | | | | | | |
|---|---|---|---|---|---|---|---|---|---|

# 面　miàn　face

面目　miànmù　face
水面　shuǐmiàn　water surface
面包　miàobāo　bread

古代"面"字像一个人面部的轮廓,中间是只眼睛。
The ancient form of "面" shows the form of a head with one eye prominently displayed in the center.

| 一 | 丆 | 厂 | 丙 | 而 | 而 | 面 | 面 | | |
|---|---|---|---|---|---|---|---|---|---|
| 面 | | | | | | | | | |

# 自　zì　self

自己　zìjǐ　oneself
自动　zìdòng　automatic
自然　zìrán　natural

古代"自"字像人鼻子的形状。
The ancient form of "自" shows a nose seen from the front.

| ′ | 亻 | 冇 | 白 | 自 | 自 | | | | |
|---|---|---|---|---|---|---|---|---|---|
| 自 | | | | | | | | | |

身　　　　　　shēn　body

身体　shēntǐ　body
身子　shēnzi　body
自身　zìshēn　self

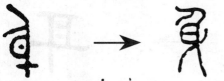

古代"身"字像一腹部很突出、怀有身孕的妇女侧立的样子。
The ancient form of "身" shows a human body with a large belly, i.e. a pregnant woman in profile.

| ' | ⼁ | ⼁ | ⼁ | 自 | 自 | 身 | | | |
|---|---|---|---|---|---|---|---|---|---|

| 身 | | | | | | | | | |
|---|---|---|---|---|---|---|---|---|---|

舟　　　　　　zhōu　boat

泛舟　fànzhōu　go boating
木已成舟　It's very late.
mù yǐ chéng zhōu

 →  → 舟

古代"舟"字像一条船的形状。
The ancient form of "舟" clearly resembles a boat.

| ' | ⼁ | 力 | 舟 | 舟 | 舟 | | | | |
|---|---|---|---|---|---|---|---|---|---|

| 舟 | | | | | | | | | |
|---|---|---|---|---|---|---|---|---|---|

耳       ěr   ear

| 耳朵 | ěrduo | ear |
| 耳闻 | ěrwén | hear of |
| 耳机 | ěrjī | earphone |

→ 耳 → 耳

古代"耳"字像从侧面看一只耳朵的形状。
The ancient form of "耳" looks like an ear.

| 一 | 厂 | 厂 | 丆 | 耳 | 耳 | | | | |
|---|---|---|---|---|---|---|---|---|---|
| 耳 | | | | | | | | | |


互       hù   mutual

| 互相 | hùxiāng | each other |
| 相互 | xiānghù | mutual |
| 互助 | hùzhù | help each other |

互 → 互

古代"互"字像一种工具使绳子绞在一起的样子。
The ancient form of "互" shows a tool for twisting ropes together.

| 一 | エ | 万 | 互 | | | | | | |
|---|---|---|---|---|---|---|---|---|---|
| 互 | | | | | | | | | |

40

欠　　qiàn　yawn, owe

| | | |
|---|---|---|
| 呵欠 | hēqiàn | yawn |
| 欠身 | qiànshēn | raise slightly |
| 欠缺 | qiànquē | be short of; deficiency |

古代"欠"字像跪坐的人仰头张口呼气。
The ancient form of "欠" shows a kneeling man raising his head, opening his mouth and breathing out.

| ノ | 亇 | 尹 | 欠 | | | | | | |
|---|---|---|---|---|---|---|---|---|---|

| 欠 | | | | | | | | | |
|---|---|---|---|---|---|---|---|---|---|

革　　gé　leather, hide

| | | |
|---|---|---|
| 皮革 | pígé | leather |
| 革除 | géchú | abolish |
| 革命 | gémìng | revolution |

古代"革"字像一张剥下的兽皮,张开着。
The ancient form of "革" shows an animal skin that has been removed from the body and spread out.

| 一 | 十 | 艹 | 艹 | 艹 | 苎 | 苎 | 莒 | 革 | |
|---|---|---|---|---|---|---|---|---|---|

| 革 | | | | | | | | | |
|---|---|---|---|---|---|---|---|---|---|

衣　　yī　clothing, clothes

衣服　yīfu　clothing
毛衣　máoyī　woolen sweater
大衣　dàyī　overcoat

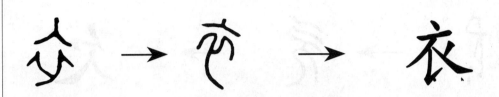

古代"衣"字像一件上衣,上面是领子,两边开口的地方是袖子,下面是衣服的下摆。
The ancient form of "衣" shows a traditional Chinese upper garment, the uppermost is the collar, the two open sides the sleeves, and the lower-half the lower hem.

| 、 | 亠 | 𠤤 | 𧘇 | 衣 | 衣 | | | | |
|---|---|---|---|---|---|---|---|---|---|
| 衣 | | | | | | | | | |

老　　lǎo　old

老人　lǎorén　old man
老师　lǎoshī　teacher
老大　lǎodà　eldest child

古代"老"字像一个老人的形象,驼着背,拄着拐杖。
The ancient form of "老" shows an old man with a stick in hand, and the back is bent from old age.

| 一 | 十 | 土 | 耂 | 老 | 老 | | | | |
|---|---|---|---|---|---|---|---|---|---|
| 老 | | | | | | | | | |

# 西   xī   west

西边　xībiān　the west
西方　xīfāng　the Occident
西餐　xīcān　Western-style food

古代"西"字像一只鸟落在巢上。鸟回巢是在夕阳"西"下的时候。

The ancient form of "西" shows a bird returning to its nest at the time when the sun sets in the west.

| 一 | 厂 | 冋 | 丙 | 西 | 西 | | | | |
|---|---|---|---|---|---|---|---|---|---|
| 西 | | | | | | | | | |

# 足   zú   foot, leg, sufficient

足球　zúqiú　football
足迹　zújì　footmark
足够　zúgòu　sufficient

古代"足"字像脚的形状,字的上部是脚腕,下部是脚面和脚趾。

The ancient form of "足" shows a foot, the upper part representing the ankle, and the lower part the instep and the toes.

| 丶 | 口 | 口 | 口 | 尸 | 早 | 尺 | 足 | | |
|---|---|---|---|---|---|---|---|---|---|
| 足 | | | | | | | | | |

两　　　liǎng　two, both

两个　　liǎnggè　two
两边　　liǎngbiān　both sides
两头　　liǎngtóu　both ends

古代"两"字像两个形状一样的东西并排着，以表示成双的东西。
The ancient form of "两" looks like two things of the same kind next to each other, signalling "a pair of".

| 一 | 厂 | 历 | 丙 | 丙 | 两 | 两 | | | |
|---|---|---|---|---|---|---|---|---|---|

| 两 | | | | | | | | | |
|---|---|---|---|---|---|---|---|---|---|

雨　　　yǔ　rain

下雨　　xiàyǔ　to rain
大雨　　dàyǔ　a heavy rain
雨衣　　yǔyī　raincoat

古代"雨"字像下雨的样子，上端一横表示天空，下面是下落的雨点。
The ancient form of "雨" shows raindrops falling from the sky represented by the upper horizontal stroke.

| 一 | 厂 | 闩 | 币 | 币 | 雨 | 雨 | 雨 | | |
|---|---|---|---|---|---|---|---|---|---|

| 雨 | | | | | | | | | |
|---|---|---|---|---|---|---|---|---|---|

肉　　　ròu　meat

| 羊肉 | yángròu | mutton |
| 牛肉 | niúròu | beef |
| 猪肉 | zhūròu | pork |

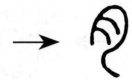 →  →

古代"肉"字像一块割下来的肉。
The ancient form of "肉" shows a piece of meat.

| 丨 | 冂 | 内 | 内 | 肉 | 肉 | | | | |
|---|---|---|---|---|---|---|---|---|---|
| 肉 | | | | | | | | | |

典　　　diǎn　standard, law

| 词典 | cídiǎn | dictionary |
| 字典 | zìdiǎn | dictionary |
| 典礼 | diǎnlǐ | ceremony |

 →  →

古代"典"字像书册放在"几"上，表示这是重要的文献或书籍。
The ancient form of "典" looks like bamboo slips on a small table(几), signalling important documents or books.

| 丨 | 冂 | 曰 | 且 | 曲 | 曲 | 典 | 典 | | |
|---|---|---|---|---|---|---|---|---|---|
| 典 | | | | | | | | | |

虎　　　　　　　hǔ　tiger

| 老虎 | lǎohǔ | tiger |
| 虎口 | hǔkǒu | jaws of death |
| 马虎 | mǎhu | careless |

 →  → 虎

古代"虎"字像一只老虎的样子，嘴张开，露着锋利的牙齿，身上是老虎特有的条纹。
The ancient form of "虎" shows a tiger with stripes on its coat and fangs in its wide open mouth.

| ' | ⺊ | ⺊ | 뉴 | 虍 | 虍 | 虍 | 虎 | | |

| 虎 | | | | | | | | | |

食　　　　　　　shí　meal, food

| 食物 | shíwù | food |
| 食品 | shípǐn | foodstuff |
| 食堂 | shítáng | canteen |

 → 食 → 食

古代"食"字像一个有盖子的盛有食物的器皿。
The ancient form of "食" a food container with its lid above the food inside.

| ノ | 八 | 亼 | 今 | 今 | 今 | 食 | 食 | 食 | |

| 食 | | | | | | | | | |

**gāo** tall, high

高大　gāodà　tall and big
高山　gāoshān　high mountain
高兴　gāoxìng　glad

 →  →

古代"高"字像一座高高的楼阁，上部是尖顶，中间是城楼，下层的建筑物中还有一个门。
The ancient form of "高" shows a two-storeyed building with a pitched roof, upstairs, and downstairs with a door in the middle.

| 、 | 亠 | 亠 | 亠 | 亠 | 亠 | 高 | 高 | 高 | 高 |
|---|---|---|---|---|---|---|---|---|---|
| 高 | | | | | | | | | |

 **xiàng** elephant, shape

大象　dàxiàng　elephant
现象　xiànxiàng　phenomenon
气象　qìxiàng　meteorology

→  →

古代"象"字像一头大象的样子，长长的鼻子和宽大身躯。
The ancient form of "象" shows an elephant, with its long nose and big body.

| ⺈ | ⺈ | ⺈ | ⺈ | ⺈ | 写 | 争 | 争 | 象 | 象 | 象 |
|---|---|---|---|---|---|---|---|---|---|---|
| 象 | | | | | | | | | | |

# 4

# INDEPENDENT CHARACTERS (2) – INDICATIVE CHARACTERS

### 指事字

用笔画的组合提示出某种抽象的意义,这种独体字叫指事字。指事字比象形字少得多。

### Indicative characters

Strokes can be combined to show an abstract meaning. Characters composed in this way are called: indicative characters. The indicative characters are much fewer in number than the pictograms.

中     zhōng    centre, middle

| 中午 | zhōngwǔ | noon |
| 中间 | zhōngjiān | among |
| 中学 | zhōngxué | middle school |

古代"中"字像一根旗杆上飘扬着旗子。中间的一竖指示这儿为正中央。

The ancient form of "中" looks like banners flying in the wind on a mast, representing the center.

上　**shàng**　up, upper, above

上边　shàngbiān　above
上午　shàngwǔ　morning
上班　shàngbān　go to work

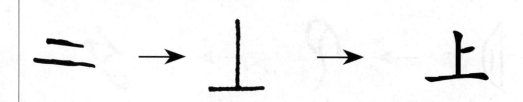

古代"上"字写成两横,底下的一横表示基线,上面的短横指示位置所在。

The ancient form of "上" is composed of two horizontal strokes, the one below standing for the base, and the shorter one above indicating the position above.

| 丨 | 卜 | 上 |  |  |  |  |  |  |  |
|---|---|---|---|---|---|---|---|---|---|
| 上 |  |  |  |  |  |  |  |  |  |

下　**xià**　down, lower, under

下边　xiàbiān　under
下午　xiàwǔ　afternoon
下班　xiàbān　come off work

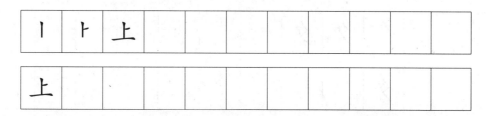

古代"下"字写成两横,上面的一横表示基线,下面的短横指示位置所在。

The ancient form of "下" is also composed of two horizontal strokes, the one above standing for the base, and the shorter one below indicating the position below.

| 一 | 丁 | 下 |  |  |  |  |  |  |  |
|---|---|---|---|---|---|---|---|---|---|
| 下 |  |  |  |  |  |  |  |  |  |

夕　　　xī　sunset

| 夕阳 | xīyáng | the setting sun |
| 夕照 | xīzhào | evening glow |
| 旦夕 | dànxī | in a short time |

 →  → 夕

古代"夕"字中间是一画(比"月"字少了一画),表示月亮只露出了一半,是傍晚时分。

The ancient form of "夕" is similar to the character 月 (moon), except that there is only one stroke inside, signalling that there is only part of a moon at that time, i.e. nightfall.

| ノ | 勹 | 夕 | | | | | | | | |
|---|---|---|---|---|---|---|---|---|---|---|

| 夕 | | | | | | | | | | |
|---|---|---|---|---|---|---|---|---|---|---|

旧 [舊]　　　jiù　past, old

| 旧日 | jiùrì | former days |
| 旧货 | jiùhuò | secondhand goods |
| 怀旧 | huáijiù | remember past times |

丨 ＋ 日 → 旧

简化字"旧"可以看成一个指事字。"日"表示日子、时间,加上左边的一竖表示时间已经过去。

This simplified form can be seem as an indicative character: "日"(sun) means day, time, and the vertical stroke added on its left means the time has passed, thus old, past.

| 丨 | 刂 | 旧 | 旧 | 旧 | | | | | | |
|---|---|---|---|---|---|---|---|---|---|---|

| 旧 | | | | | | | | | | |
|---|---|---|---|---|---|---|---|---|---|---|

tiān sky, day

| | | |
|---|---|---|
| 天空 | tiānkōng | the sky |
| 今天 | jīntiān | today |
| 天天 | tiāntiān | every day |

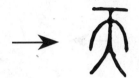 →  →

古代"天"字是一个正面站立的人,头上加了一横,表示人头顶着的是天空。
The ancient form of "天" shows a standing man with a horizontal stroke on his head to indicate that which is above his head, i.e. the sky.

| 一 | 二 | 天 | 天 | | | | | | |
|---|---|---|---|---|---|---|---|---|---|

| 天 | | | | | | | | | |
|---|---|---|---|---|---|---|---|---|---|

 tài too, excessively

| | | |
|---|---|---|
| 太大 | tài dà | too big |
| 太空 | tàikōng | the firmament |
| 太太 | tàitai | madame |

大 + 、 →

"太"字是在"大"字下边加一点,表示"过于""最、极"的意思。
This character is composed of "大" (big) with a dot added, meaning 'too, excessively'.

| 一 | ナ | 大 | 太 | | | | | | |
|---|---|---|---|---|---|---|---|---|---|

| 太 | | | | | | | | | |
|---|---|---|---|---|---|---|---|---|---|

51

本　　běn　root, basis, original

| 本来 | běnlái | original |
| 根本 | gēnběn | basic |
| 本人 | běnrén | myself |

古代"本"字在"木"字下面加上一横,指示这儿是树的根。

The ancient form of "本" is derived from "木" (tree) to which a horizontal stroke has been added to signify the root.

| 一 | 十 | 才 | 木 | 本 | | | | | |
|---|---|---|---|---|---|---|---|---|---|

| 本 | | | | | | | | | |
|---|---|---|---|---|---|---|---|---|---|

末　　mò　tip, end

| 末尾 | mòwěi | end |
| 末日 | mòrì | doom |
| 周末 | zhōumò | weekend |

古代"末"字是在"木"字上端加一横,指示这儿是树木的"末梢"。

The ancient form of "末" is also based on "木" (tree) with a stroke added to signify the top of the tree.

| 一 | 二 | 十 | 才 | 末 | | | | | |
|---|---|---|---|---|---|---|---|---|---|

| 末 | | | | | | | | | |
|---|---|---|---|---|---|---|---|---|---|

片　　piàn　a flat, thin piece

| 刀片 | dāopiàn | blade |
| 肉片 | ròupiàn | sliced meat |
| 照片 | zhàopiàn | photograph |

片 → 片 → 片

古代"片"字是"木"()字的一半,表示这是从木头上劈下的木片。
The ancient form of "片" is one half of the pictogram "木" (tree) thus indicating a log cut vertically.

| ノ | ノ′ | 广 | 片 | | | | | | | |
|---|---|---|---|---|---|---|---|---|---|---|

| 片 | | | | | | | | | | |
|---|---|---|---|---|---|---|---|---|---|---|

元　　yuán　first, chief, basic

| 元旦 | yuándàn | New Year's Day |
| 元月 | yuányuè | January |
| 美元 | měiyuán | U.S dollar |

元 → 元 → 元

古代"元"字像一侧立的人,上面两横指示这儿是头。
The ancient form of "元" shows the profile of a man standing up; the two horizontal strokes show his head.

| 一 | 二 | 于 | 元 | | | | | | | |
|---|---|---|---|---|---|---|---|---|---|---|

| 元 | | | | | | | | | | |
|---|---|---|---|---|---|---|---|---|---|---|

53

xuè blood

血压　　xuèyā　　　blood pressure
血液　　xuèyè　　　blood
血型　　xuèxíng　　blood group

中国古代祭祀时把血放到器皿中，古代"血"字是"皿"（器皿）字上加一点，指示里边盛的是血。

In ancient times, the sacrificial blood was put in a receptacle; this is why the character "血" comes from "皿" (receptacle) to which has been added an angled stroke to indicate that there's blood inside.

| ノ | 亻 | 白 | 血 | 血 | 血 | | | | |
|---|---|---|---|---|---|---|---|---|---|
| 血 | | | | | | | | | |

 yán speech, word

语言　　yǔyán　　　language
方言　　fāngyán　　dialect
言行　　yánxíng　　words and deeds

 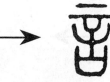  

古代"言"字像从嘴里伸出的舌头，舌头上加了一横，表示从这儿发出的声音。

The ancient form of "言" shows a tongue coming out of a mouth, the stroke added to the tongue indicates that sound is produced here.

| 、 | 二 | 亠 | 言 | 言 | 言 | 言 | | | |
|---|---|---|---|---|---|---|---|---|---|
| 言 | | | | | | | | | |

## 合体字(上)—会意字

### COMBINED CHARACTERS (1)— ASSOCIATIVE CHARACTERS

**5**

**会意字**

会意字是一种合体字。由两个或两个以上偏旁所表示的意义合在一起来表示新的意义的合体字叫会意字。

**偏旁**

构成合体字的部分叫偏旁,合体字的偏旁有的是个独体字,有的是合体字,有的是由独体字演变而成的符号。如"亻"就是由人字演变而成的一个的符号。

**合体字的结构**

偏旁在字中所占的部位不同,使合体字形成三种主要结构,即:左右结构、上下结构、内外结构。本讲,我们按照结构的类型来介绍会意字。

### Associative characters

Associative characters are one kind of combined characters. They result from the combination of two or more elements to create a new character with a new meaning.

### Elements

The parts which form the combined characters are called elements. The elements are either independent characters, combined characters or symbols derived from the independent characters, e.g. "亻" is a symbol derived from the pictogram "人".

### The structure of combined characters

According to the position of the element, the structures of the combined characters are divided into three principal types: left-right sturcture, top-bottom structure, in-out structure. This chapter presents the associative characters in terms of their structural types.

# 【左右结构(一)】

**LEFT – RIGHT STRUCTURE (1)**

左右两部分相等,书写顺序是:先左,后右。

Two equal parts, order of writing：first left，then right.

| 明 | | | | 明天 | míngtiān | tomorrow |
| --- | --- | --- | --- | --- | --- | --- |
| | míng | bright, light, clear | | 明年 | míngnián | next year |
| | | | | 明白 | míngbai | understand |

日 ＋ 月 → 明

白天和夜晚"日"和"月"给人们带来光明,两字合在一起表示光明。

Day and night "sun"（日）and "moon"（月）bring bright light to people. The two together mean 'bright'.

| 丨 | 冂 | 月 | 日 | 刞 | 明 | 明 | 明 | | | |
| --- | --- | --- | --- | --- | --- | --- | --- | --- | --- | --- |

| 明 | | | | | | | | | | |
| --- | --- | --- | --- | --- | --- | --- | --- | --- | --- | --- |

**lín　forest**

| 树林 | shùlín | forest |
|------|--------|--------|
| 森林 | sēnlín | full of trees |
| 林业 | línyè | forestry |

木　+　木　→　林

"木"表示树,两棵树并排在一起表示树木很多,很多树在一起就成"树林"了。

"木" means tree, two trees together signal that there are a lot of trees, i.e. a forest.

| 一 | 十 | 才 | 木 | 术 | 杧 | 材 | 林 | | | |
|---|---|---|---|---|---|---|---|---|---|---|
| 林 | | | | | | | | | | |

 **cóng　follow, from**

| 服从 | fúcóng | obey |
|------|--------|------|
| 从前 | cóngqián | before |
| 从事 | cóngshì | go in for |

人　+　人　→　从

"从"是两个"人"字合在一起,一个人在前,一人在后,表示跟随的意思。

The character "从" is an association of two characters "人" (man), one behind the other, signifying that a person is following the other.

| 丿 | 人 | 丛 | 从 | | | | | | | |
|---|---|---|---|---|---|---|---|---|---|---|
| 从 | | | | | | | | | | |

好　　　hǎo　　good, fine

| 好人 | hǎorén | good person |
| 好看 | hǎokàn | good-looking |
| 很好 | hěnhǎo | very good |

女　+　子　→　好

"女"指女人，"子"指孩子，"女人"有了"孩子"是件"好"事。
"女" means a woman, "子" means a child. For a woman who has a child is a "good" thing.

| ㇛ | ㇛ | 女 | 好 | 好 | 好 | | | | |
|---|---|---|---|---|---|---|---|---|---|

| 好 | | | | | | | | | |
|---|---|---|---|---|---|---|---|---|---|

妇[婦]　fù　　married woman

| 妇女 | fùnǚ | woman |
| 夫妇 | fūfù | husband and wife |
| 妇科 | fùkē | gynaecology |

女　+　ㅋ　→　妇

"ㅋ"是"帚"的简写。"帚"指扫帚，一个女人手持扫帚扫地，是位"妇女"的形象。
"ㅋ" is the simplified form of "帚" (broom). The character shows a woman sweeping the floor with a broom, thus, a married woman.

| ㇛ | ㇛ | 女 | 妇 | 妇 | 妇 | | | | |
|---|---|---|---|---|---|---|---|---|---|

| 妇 | | | | | | | | | |
|---|---|---|---|---|---|---|---|---|---|

58

# 如

**rú** in compliance, as

如下　rúxià　as follows
如此　rúcǐ　like that
如果　rúguǒ　if

女 + 口 → 如

中国古代，"女子"对出自丈夫之"口"的话是要绝对服从的。
In ancient times, a woman had to obey every word issuing from her husband's mouth.

| く | 乆 | 女 | 女 | 如 | 如 | | | | |
|---|---|---|---|---|---|---|---|---|---|

| 如 | | | | | | | | | |
|---|---|---|---|---|---|---|---|---|---|

# 利

**lì** sharp, benefit

锋利　fēnglì　sharp
流利　liúlì　fluent
利用　lìyòng　use

禾 + 刂 → 利

"禾"是庄稼，"刂"是"刀"字的变体，可以割庄稼的刀是锋利的。
"禾" depicts the stalk of a crop；"刂" is a variant of "刀" (knife)；the knives used for cutting crops are very sharp.

| ノ | 二 | 千 | 禾 | 禾 | 利 | 利 | | | |
|---|---|---|---|---|---|---|---|---|---|

| 利 | | | | | | | | | |
|---|---|---|---|---|---|---|---|---|---|

59

# 双

shuāng    pair, even, both

双人床    shuāngrénchuáng    double bed
双方      shuāngfāng          both sides
一双      yī shuāng           one pair

又 + 又 → 双

"又"古文字中表示一只手,两只手在一起叫一"双"手,现泛指成双的东西。

The ancient form of "又" shows a hand; two hands together mean a pair.

| ﾌ | 又 | 双 | 双 | | | | | | |
|---|---|---|---|---|---|---|---|---|---|

| 双 | | | | | | | | | |
|---|---|---|---|---|---|---|---|---|---|

# 取

qǔ    take, get, fetch

取得    qǔdé      gain
取代    qǔdài     replace
争取    zhēngqǔ   strive for

耳 + 又 → 取

"耳"指耳朵,"又"是表示手,中国古代以割取敌人耳朵作为计数献功的方式,后泛指获取的意思。

"耳" shows an ear; "又" shows a hand. In ancient times the enemies' ears were proof of one's military achievements. A hand holding an ear is used to denote "to take" in a general sense.

| 一 | 厂 | 厅 | 斤 | 耳 | 耳 | 取 | 取 | | |
|---|---|---|---|---|---|---|---|---|---|

| 取 | | | | | | | | | |
|---|---|---|---|---|---|---|---|---|---|

朝     **zhāo**    dawn

| 朝阳 | zhāoyáng | morning sun |
|---|---|---|
| 朝夕 | zhāoxī | day and night |
| 朝气 | zhāoqì | vigour |

卓 + 月 → 朝

太阳已从草丛中升起，月亮还没落下的时候。

The moment when the sun appears on the horizon , the moon has not yet disppeared.

| 一 | 十 | 卉 | 古 | 古 | 直 | 卓 | 車 | 朝 | 朝 | |
|---|---|---|---|---|---|---|---|---|---|---|

| 朝 | | | | | | | | | | |

解     **jiě**    separate, untie

| 解剖 | jiěpōu | dissect |
|---|---|---|
| 解开 | jiěkāi | untie |
| 解决 | jiějué | solve |

角 + 刀 + 牛 → 解

用刀把牛角剖开，后来泛指剖开、分解的意思。

A knife（刀）is used to cut open a bull's horns(牛角), therefore "解" signifies to cut open or to separate.

| ′ | ″ | ⌐ | 尸 | 角 | 角 | 角 | 𧢲 | 𧢲 | 解 | |
|---|---|---|---|---|---|---|---|---|---|---|

| 解 | | | | | | | | | | |

# 【左右结构(二)】

## LEFT – RIGHT STRUCTURE (2)

左小,右大,书写顺序也是:先左,后右。

Small left part, large right part, order of writing: Left first, then right.

休     xiū    rest, stop

| | | |
|---|---|---|
| 休息 | xiūxi | have a rest |
| 休假 | xiūjià | have a vacation |
| 休养 | xiūyǎng | recuperate |

"亻"是人字的变体,"木"表示一棵树,人靠着树是在休息。

"亻" is a variant of "人", "木" shows a tree. A person leaning against a tree signifies "to have a rest".

| ノ | 亻 | 亻 | 什 | 休 | 休 | | | | |
|---|---|---|---|---|---|---|---|---|---|

| 休 | | | | | | | | | |
|---|---|---|---|---|---|---|---|---|---|

体      tǐ   body

| 身体 | shēntǐ | body |
| 人体 | réntǐ | human body |
| 体力 | tǐlì | physical power |

亻 + 本 → 体

"亻"是人,"本"是根本,身体是人之本。

"亻" means man ; "本" means root. The body is the root of every man's being.

| 亻 | 本 | | | | | | | | |
|---|---|---|---|---|---|---|---|---|---|
| 体 | | | | | | | | | |


信      xìn   trust, letter

| 相信 | xiānxìn | believe |
| 信封 | xìnfēng | envelope |
| 信纸 | xìnzhǐ | letter paper |

亻 + 言 → 信

"亻"是人,"言"是语言,人说话诚实才会让人信任。

"亻" means man; "言" means language. When you speak truthfully, the others will trust you.

| ノ | 亻 | 亻 | 亼 | 信 | 信 | 信 | 信 | 信 | |
|---|---|---|---|---|---|---|---|---|---|
| 信 | | | | | | | | | |

# 位 wèi place, position

| | | |
|---|---|---|
| 座位 | zuòwèi | seat |
| 位置 | wèizhì | position |
| 位子 | wèizi | seat |

亻 + 立 → 位

“亻”是人,“立”是站立,人站立需要一个位置。

“亻” means man; “立” means upright. 位 refers to the position where a man stands.

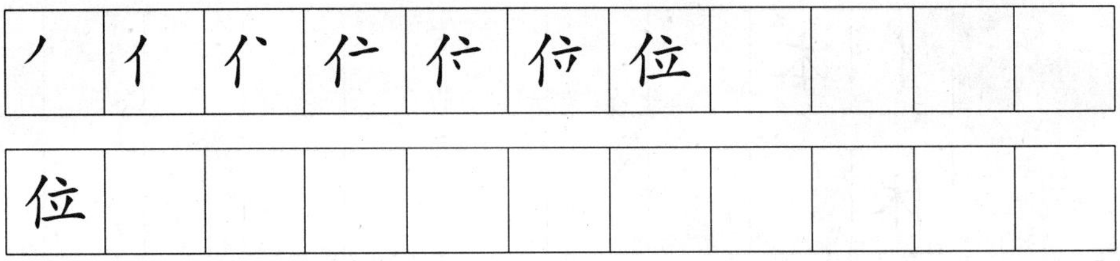

# 冰 bīng ice

| | | |
|---|---|---|
| 结冰 | jiébīng | freeze |
| 滑冰 | huábīng | skate |
| 冰山 | bīngshān | iceberg |

冫 + 水 → 冰

偏旁“冫”,表示液体遇冷凝结的样子,水遇冷凝结成冰。

“冫” is the element of cold; “水” means water. Water turns into ice, at a result of great cold.

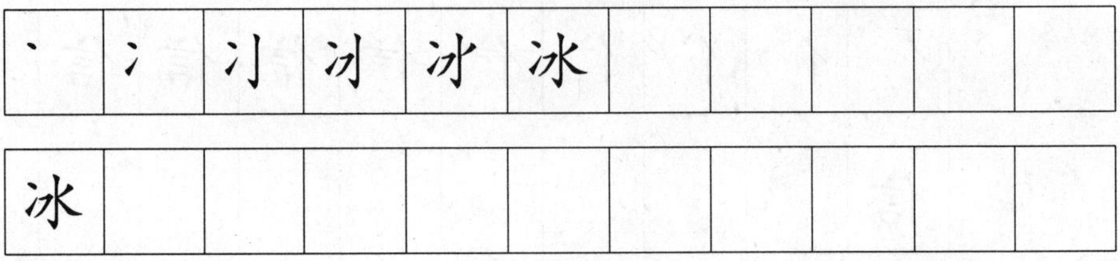

泪　　　　lèi　tear

眼泪　yǎnlèi　tears
泪水　lèishuǐ　tear
流泪　liúlèi　shed tears

氵 ＋ 目 → 泪

"氵"是水字旁，"目"是眼睛，眼睛里流出的液体就是泪。

The element "氵" means water; "目" represents an eye. Water running from the eyes is called tears.

| 丶 | 丶 | 氵 | 汀 | 汩 | 汩 | 泪 | 泪 | | |
|---|---|---|---|---|---|---|---|---|---|
| 泪 | | | | | | | | | |

汽　　　　qì　steam, vapour

汽车　qìchē　automobile
汽水　qìshuǐ　soda water
汽油　qìyóu　petrol

氵 ＋ 气 → 汽

"氵"是水字旁，"气"指气体，由水变成的气体是水蒸气。

The element "氵" means water; "气" means gas. Gas evaporating from water is known as steam.

| 丶 | 丶 | 氵 | 氵 | 汽 | 汽 | 汽 | | | |
|---|---|---|---|---|---|---|---|---|---|
| 汽 | | | | | | | | | |

沙　　　　shā　sand

沙子　shāzi　sand
沙漠　shāmò　desert
沙滩　shātān　sandy beach

氵 + 少 → 沙

"氵"是个偏旁，表示水。水少了才可以看到河底的沙子。

"氵" is the element of water; "少" means few. In a shallow river we can see the sand at the bottom.

| 丶 | 氵 | 氵 | 氵丿 | 氵少 | 氵少 | 沙 | | | |
|---|---|---|---|---|---|---|---|---|---|

| 沙 | | | | | | | | | |
|---|---|---|---|---|---|---|---|---|---|

酒　　　jiǔ　alcoholic drink

酒杯　jiūbēi　glass
酒吧　jiūbā　bar
白酒　báijiǔ　spirits

氵 + 酉 → 酒

"氵"是水字旁，"酉"是盛酒的器皿，酒罐里的液体就是酒。

"氵" means water; "酉" represents a receptacle containing alcohol. The liquid in the container is alcohol.

| 丶 | 氵 | 氵 | 氵 | 沪 | 沔 | 沔 | 洒 | 酒 | 酒 |
|---|---|---|---|---|---|---|---|---|---|

| 酒 | | | | | | | | | |
|---|---|---|---|---|---|---|---|---|---|

66

# 阳 [陽]　yáng　sun, positive

太阳　　tàiyáng　　sun
阳光　　yángguāng　sunlight
阳性　　yángxìng　　positive

阝 + 日 → 阳

偏旁"阝"表示土山,"日"表示太阳,山有太阳的一面为阳面。
The element "阝" means a hill; "日" means the sun. The two together show the sunny face of a mountain.

| 阝 | 阝 | 阝 | 阴 | 阳 | | | | | |
|---|---|---|---|---|---|---|---|---|---|

| 阳 | | | | | | | | | |
|---|---|---|---|---|---|---|---|---|---|

# 阴 [陰]　yīn　overcast, shade

阴天　　yīntiān　　overcast sky
阴暗　　yīn'àn　　dark
阴阳　　yīnyáng　　Yin and Yang

阝 + 月 → 阴

偏旁"阝"表示土山,山背阴的地方,就像月光下一样阴暗。
The element "阝" means a hill; "月" means the moon. At the side of a hill where the sun can't reach, it is as dark as under the moonlight.

| 阝 | 阝 | 阝 | 阴 | 阴 | 阴 | | | | |
|---|---|---|---|---|---|---|---|---|---|

| 阴 | | | | | | | | | |
|---|---|---|---|---|---|---|---|---|---|

# 嫁 jià （of a woman）marry

嫁人　jiàrén　get married
出嫁　chūjià　get married
嫁妆　jiàzhuāng dowry

女 ＋ 家 → 嫁

"女"指女子，"家"是家庭的意思。中国女子结婚以后去男方家，所以叫出嫁。

"女" means a woman; "家" means the family household. Once married, a Chinese woman goes to live in her husband's house.

| 女 | 女 | 女 | 圹 | 圹 | 圹 | 娩 | 娧 | 嫁 | 嫁 | 嫁 |
|---|---|---|---|---|---|---|---|---|---|---|

| 嫁 | | | | | | | | | | |
|---|---|---|---|---|---|---|---|---|---|---|

# 睡 shuì sleep

睡觉　shuìjiào　sleep
睡眠　shuìmián　sleep
瞌睡　kēshuì　sleepy

目 ＋ 垂 → 睡

"目"是眼睛，"垂"是下垂的意思，眼睑下垂是要睡觉的样子。

"目" means eye; "垂" means falling. When the eyelids drop, a person is ready to go to sleep.

| 目 | 目 | 目 | 目 | 睅 | 睡 | 睡 | 睡 | | |
|---|---|---|---|---|---|---|---|---|---|

| 睡 | | | | | | | | | |
|---|---|---|---|---|---|---|---|---|---|

# 【左右结构（三）】

## LEFT – RIGHT STRUCTURE (3)

左大，右小，书写顺序也是：先左，后右。

Large left part, small right part, order of writing：Left first, then right.

删　　shān　delete, leave out

| 删除 | shānchú | delete |
| 删改 | shāngǎi | revise |
| 删节 | shānjié | abridge |

册 ＋ 刂 → 删

古代"册"字表示用竹简作成的书，"刂"指"刀"。古时要用"刀"才能把刻在竹简上的字删去。

The ancient form of "册" looks like many bamboo slips tied together, and "刂" represents "knife". In ancient times a knife was used to erase the characters on a bamboo slip, thus, "to delete".

| 丿 | 刀 | 刪 | 刪 | 册 | 删 | 删 | | | |
|---|---|---|---|---|---|---|---|---|---|

| 删 | | | | | | | | | |
|---|---|---|---|---|---|---|---|---|---|

# 【上下结构(一)】

## TOP – BOTTOM STRUCTURE (1)

上下两部分相等,书写顺序是:先上,后下。

Two equal parts, order of writing: Top first, then bottom.

| 美 | měi  beautiful | 美丽 | měili | beautiful |
| --- | --- | --- | --- | --- |
| | | 美人 | měirén | beautiful woman |
| | | 美国 | Měiguó | U.S.A |

羊 + 大 → 美

古人以羊肉为主要食品。"羊"肥"大",则肉味鲜"美"。

"羊" shows a sheep, "大" means big. Mutton was the main food in ancient times. If a sheep is big, the mutton in delicious.

| 、 | 丷 | 丷 | 丷 | 半 | 羊 | 美 | 美 | 美 | |
| --- | --- | --- | --- | --- | --- | --- | --- | --- | --- |

| 美 | | | | | | | | | |
| --- | --- | --- | --- | --- | --- | --- | --- | --- | --- |

70

歪 **wāi** askew, crooked

| | | |
|---|---|---|
| 歪斜. | wāixié | crooked |
| 歪曲 | wāiqū | distort |
| 歪风 | wāifēng | evil wind |

不 + 正 → 歪

"不"是否定的意思，"正"是正中的意思，不正就是歪了。

"不" means no; "正" means straight. What is not straight is askew.

一 丆 才 不 歪 歪 歪 歪 歪

歪

甭 **béng** don't, needn't

| | | |
|---|---|---|
| 甭去 | béngqù | don't go |
| 甭说 | béngshuō | don't say |
| 甭买 | béngmǎi | don't buy |

不 + 用 → 甭

"甭"就是"不用"的意思。

" 甭" means "there is no need to ".

一 丆 才 不 不 甮 甮 甮 甭

甭

71

尖　jiān　point, tip

尖刀　jiāndāo　sharp knife
尖端　jiānduān　most advanced
尖子　jiānzi　the best of its kind

小　+　大　→　尖

　　尖的东西，形状是上面小，下面大，所以"小"字在上，"大"字在下，表示尖的意思。
"小" means small; "大" means big. Pointed objects are narrow at the top and broad at the bottom.

丨　小　小　少　少　尖

尖

尘　chén　dust, dirt

尘土　chéntǔ　dust
灰尘　huīchén　dust, dirt
粉尘　fěnchén　powder

小　+　土　→　尘

　　小的土是灰尘，所以用"小"加"土"表示灰尘。
"小" means small; "土" means soil. Dust consists of small particles of soil.

丨　小　小　少　少　尘

尘

劣　　liè　bad, inferior

恶劣　èliè　odious
劣等　lièděng　of inferior quality
劣迹　lièjì　misdeed

少　＋　力　→　劣

"少"是数量不多的意思，"力"是力量，干活少出力，被认为是不好的。

"少" means few; "力" means strength; Working without exerting oneself is regarded as bad.

| 丶 | 小 | 小 | 少 | 少 | 劣 | | | | |
|---|---|---|---|---|---|---|---|---|---|
| 劣 | | | | | | | | | |

男　　nán　man, male

男人　nánrén　man
男子　nánzǐ　man; male
男性　nánxìng　the male sex

男　＋　力　→　男

"田"是田地，"力"是力气，在田地里工作的人，一般都是男人，因为他们有力气。

"田" means field; "力" means strength. People that work in the fields are generally men because they have strength.

| 丶 | 冂 | 曰 | 田 | 田 | 甼 | 男 | | | |
|---|---|---|---|---|---|---|---|---|---|
| 男 | | | | | | | | | |

73

分　fēn　divide, separate

| 分开 | fēnkāi | separate |
| 分别 | fēnbié | leave each other |
| 区分 | qūfēn | differentiate |

用"刀"在物体的中间一切，可以把它分成两半。

"八" signifies separation; "刀" means a knife. Something cut by a knife is separated.

| ノ | 八 | 分 | 分 | | | | | |

| 分 | | | | | | | | |

公　gōng　fair, public

| 公平 | gōngpíng | fair |
| 公道 | gōngdào | justice |
| 公共 | gōnggòng | public |

八 ＋ ム →

"八"有违背的意思，"ム"表示"私"，与"私"相违背就是"公"。

"八" means contrary, "ム" means private. Public is the opposite of private.

| ノ | 八 | 公 | 公 | | | | | |

| 公 | | | | | | | | |

合    hé   close, join

| 合上 | héshang | close |
| 合作 | hézuò | cooperate |
| 联合 | liánhé | unite |

人 ＋ 口 → 合

"人"表示三面闭合的意思,加上"口"字,表示合拢就像把口闭上一样。

"人" means three sides together form an enclosure, and "口" (mouth) is added to indicate the enclosure is formed in the way as one closes his mouth.

| ノ | 人 | 亼 | 仒 | 合 | 合 | | | |

| 合 | | | | | | | | |

拿    ná   take, hold

| 拿来 | nálái | bring it here |
| 拿着 | názhe | be holding |
| 拿手 | náshǒu | be good at |

合 ＋ 手 → 拿

拿东西的动作是把"手""合"起来。

"合" means close; "手" means hand. We close our hands to take something.

| ノ | 人 | 人 | 仒 | 合 | 合 | 仚 | 仚 | 仚 | 拿 |

| 拿 | | | | | | | | |

75

采 　　　　　**cǎi　pick**

采摘　cǎizhāi　pick
采取　cǎiqǔ　adopt
采用　cǎiyòng　use

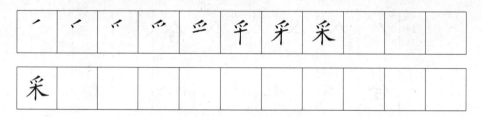

"爫"像一只手背朝上的手，"木"是树木，手在树上采摘果实。

"爫"is a hand with the palm downward, and "木" shows a tree. A hand on a tree indicates picking up fruits.

| ノ | ⺈ | ⺈ | 爫 | 平 | 乎 | 采 | 采 | | | |
|---|---|---|---|---|---|---|---|---|---|---|

| 采 | | | | | | | | | | |
|---|---|---|---|---|---|---|---|---|---|---|

名　　　　　**míng　name**

名字　míngzi　name
姓名　xíngmíng　full name
有名　yǒumíng　famous

夕 ＋ 口 → 名

"夕"指晚上，晚上招呼人，看不见，应张口呼其"名"。

"夕" means the setting sun, thus, nightfall. " 口" means mouth. At nightfall, in order to greet someone you have to open your mouth to call his name "名" because you cannot see him clearly.

| ノ | ク | 夕 | 夕 | 名 | 名 | | | | | |
|---|---|---|---|---|---|---|---|---|---|---|

| 名 | | | | | | | | | | |
|---|---|---|---|---|---|---|---|---|---|---|

右　　　yòu　right side

右边　　yòubiān　the right side
右面　　yòumiàn　the right side
右手　　yòushǒu　the right hand

ナ ＋ 口 → 右

"ナ"是一只手,用来帮助吃饭的那只手所代表的一方,是右边。

"ナ" depicts a hand; "口" means mouth. We use our right hand when we eat. The right hand represents the right side.

| 一 | ナ | ナ | 右 | 右 | | | | | |
|---|---|---|---|---|---|---|---|---|---|

| 右 | | | | | | | | | |
|---|---|---|---|---|---|---|---|---|---|

左　　　zuǒ　left side

左边　　zuǒbiān　the left side
左手　　zuǒshǒu　the left hand
左右　　zuǒyòu　around

ナ ＋ 工 → 左

"ナ"是一只手,用来帮助做工的那只手所代表的一方,叫左边。

"ナ" depicts a hand; "工" means work. When we work, we often have to hold a tool with our left hand. The left hand represents the left side.

| 一 | ナ | 左 | 左 | 左 | | | | | |
|---|---|---|---|---|---|---|---|---|---|

| 左 | | | | | | | | | |
|---|---|---|---|---|---|---|---|---|---|

77

友      yǒu   friend

| | | |
|---|---|---|
| 友好 | yǒuhǎo | friendly |
| 友谊 | yǒuyì | friendship |
| 朋友 | péngyǒu | friend |

ナ ＋ 又 → 友

"ナ"是一只手,"又"古文字中也表示一只手,两只手握在一起,表示友好。

"ナ" indicates a hand, the ancient form of "又" also shows a hand. The fact of one man's hand holding that of another is a sign of friendship between the two.

| 一 | ナ | 方 | 友 | | | | | | |
|---|---|---|---|---|---|---|---|---|---|

| 友 | | | | | | | | | |
|---|---|---|---|---|---|---|---|---|---|

灰      huī   ash

| | | |
|---|---|---|
| 灰尘 | huīchén | dust |
| 灰色 | huīsè | grey |
| 烟灰 | yānhuī | cigarette ash |

ナ ＋ 火 → 灰

"ナ"是一只手,在"火"字上边,表示用手把火熄灭以后看到的就是灰。

"ナ" shows a hand, "火" means fire. A fire underneath a hand signals that it has been extinguished by a hand. Once the fire is out, we can see the ashes.

| 一 | ナ | 大 | 太 | 灰 | 灰 | | | | |
|---|---|---|---|---|---|---|---|---|---|

| 灰 | | | | | | | | | |
|---|---|---|---|---|---|---|---|---|---|

早　　　zǎo　morning, early

| 早上 | zǎoshàng | morning |
| 早晨 | zǎochén | morning |
| 早安 | zǎoān | good morning |

日　+　十　→　早

　　"日"是太阳,"十"代表地面上的物体,"日"在"十"上,表示太阳刚升起的时候。
"日" means sun; "十" shows objects on the earth. The sun situated above the objects depicts the moment of sunrise.

丶　丨　冂　日　日　旦　早

早

旱　　　hàn　dry spell

| 干旱 | gānhàn | arid |
| 旱灾 | hànzāi | drought |
| 旱季 | hànjì | dry season |

日　+　干　→　旱

　　"日"是太阳,"干"有干燥的意思,天旱的时候,太阳炎热,很干燥。
"日" means sun; "干" means dry. When there's a drought, it's very hot and dry.

丶　丨　冂　日　日　旦　旦　旱

旱

# 众 [衆] zhòng many, numerous

| | | |
|---|---|---|
| 群众 | qúnzhòng | the masses |
| 观众 | guānzhòng | spectators |
| 听众 | tīngzhòn | audience |

人 + 人 + 人 → 众

"人"字表示站立的人,三个人站在一起,表示人很多,人多为"众"。

"人" is a standing man. Three men together indicate a big number of people.

| 丿 | 人 | 仒 | 仌 | 夵 | 众 | | | | |
|---|---|---|---|---|---|---|---|---|---|

| 众 | | | | | | | | | |
|---|---|---|---|---|---|---|---|---|---|

# 坐 zuò sit

| | | |
|---|---|---|
| 请坐 | qǐng zuò | Please sit down |
| 坐下 | zuòxia | sit down |
| 坐着 | zuòzhe | be sitting |

人 + 人 + 土 → 坐

古文字中,"坐"字像两个"人"坐在"土地"上。

"人" means man; "土" means soil. The ancient form of "坐" shows two men sitting on the ground.

| 丿 | 人 | 亻丿 | 从 | 坐 | 坐 | 坐 | | | |
|---|---|---|---|---|---|---|---|---|---|

| 坐 | | | | | | | | | |
|---|---|---|---|---|---|---|---|---|---|

品　　pǐn　article, grade

品种　pǐnzhǒng　variety
商品　shāngpǐn　commodity
产品　chǎnpǐn　product

口 + 口 + 口 → 品

这里的"口"字像盛东西的器皿,三个口字在一起表示器皿的品类很多。

Here "口" shows the content of a receptacle. Three "口" together signify a variety of objects.

丶 丨丁 口 口 口 品 品 品 品 品

品

见 [見]　jiàn　see, meet with

看见　kànjiàn　see
再见　zàijiàn　good-bye
见面　jiànmiàn　meet

目 + 儿 → 見 → 见

"目"是眼睛,"儿"是人字的变体,两字合在一起表示人眼所见。

"目" means eye; "儿" means man. The combination of the two indicates what a person can see.

丨 冂 贝 见

见

81

看      **kàn**    **look at**

| 看见 | kànjiàn | catch sight of |
| 看病 | kànbìng | see a doctor |
| 好看 | hǎokàn | good-looking |

手 + 目 → 看

"手"是手字的变体，"目"是眼睛，手放在眼睛上方，是在向远处眺望的样子。

"手" means hand;"目" means eye, A hand on top of an eye signals to look into the distance under the shade formed by the hand.

| 一 | 二 | 三 | 手 | 手 | 看 | 看 | 看 | 看 | | |

| 看 | | | | | | | | | | |

有      **yǒu**    **have, own**

| 有钱 | yǒuqián | rich |
| 有名 | yǒumíng | famous |
| 有事 | yǒushì | occupied |

ナ + 月 → 有

"ナ"是一只手，"月"古文字中同"肉"，手里拿着一块肉，表示已经拥有了。

"ナ" shows a hand;the ancient form of "月" sometimes means the same as "肉" (meat). Holding a piece of meat in your hands signifies owning it.

| 一 | ナ | 才 | 有 | 有 | 有 | | | | |

| 有 | | | | | | | | | |

# 里　lǐ　hometown, inside

| 乡里 | xiānglǐ | home village |
|---|---|---|
| 里弄 | lǐnòng | neighbourhood |
| 里边 | lǐbiān | inside |

田 ＋ 土 → 里

　　人们生活起居，离不开农田和土地。"里"的本义表示"居住的地方"。

"田" means field; "土" means earth. Earth and fields are so essential to our life that we cannot do with out them. "里" in sense signifies a hometown.

| 丶 | 冂 | 冖 | 日 | 甲 | 甼 | 里 | | | |
|---|---|---|---|---|---|---|---|---|---|

| 里 | | | | | | | | | |
|---|---|---|---|---|---|---|---|---|---|

# 至　zhì　to, until

| 至今 | zhìjīn | up to now |
|---|---|---|
| 至死 | zhìsǐ | up to death |
| 至于 | zhìyú | as for |

 →  →  至

　　古代"至"字是一支箭倒立着插在地上，表示从高处落到地面上。

The ancient form of "至" shows an arrow stuck in the ground, meaning something falling from above has rached its goal.

| 一 | 丆 | 云 | 至 | 至 | 至 | | | | |
|---|---|---|---|---|---|---|---|---|---|

| 至 | | | | | | | | | |
|---|---|---|---|---|---|---|---|---|---|

# 走

**zǒu  walk**

| | | |
|---|---|---|
| 走路 | zǒulù | walk |
| 走运 | zǒuyùn | be in luck |
| 走私 | zǒusī | smuggle |

土 + 止 → 走

"土"指土地,"止"是脚,人走路的时候,脚踩在地上。

"土" means earth; "止" is part of "足" (foot). When you walk your feet touch the ground.

| 土 | 丰 | 丰 | 走 | 走 | | | | | |
|---|---|---|---|---|---|---|---|---|---|

| 走 | | | | | | | | | |
|---|---|---|---|---|---|---|---|---|---|


# 是

**shì  correct, to be**

| | | |
|---|---|---|
| 是非 | shìfēi | right and wrong |
| 是否 | shìfǒu | whether or not |
| 是的 | shìde | yes |

日 + 疋 → 是

"日"指白天,"疋"是脚,表示行走。白天出门行走是正确的选择。"是"的本义是正确。

"日" signifies daytime; "疋" is part of "足" (foot), meaning walk. If someone goes out during the day, it's a good decision. "是" means correct. (At night one couldn't go out, because there was no light.)

| 丨 | 冂 | 日 | 日 | 旦 | 早 | early | 昰 | 是 | |
|---|---|---|---|---|---|---|---|---|---|

| 是 | | | | | | | | | |
|---|---|---|---|---|---|---|---|---|---|

# 娶

qǔ  marry (a woman)

娶亲　qǔqīn　get married
娶妻　qǔqī　take a wife
嫁娶　jiàqǔ　marriage

取 ＋ 女 → 娶

"取"是获得的意思，"女"指女子，男子结婚为娶。

"取" means obtaining; "女" means woman. When a man takes a woman he is getting married.

| 一 | 厂 | 兀 | 冇 | 耳 | 耳 | 取 | 取 | 聚 | 娶 | 娶 |
|---|---|---|---|---|---|---|---|---|---|---|

| 娶 | | | | | | | | | | |
|---|---|---|---|---|---|---|---|---|---|---|

# 忘

wàng  forget

遗忘　yíwàng　forget
忘记　wàngjì　forget
难忘　nánwàng　unforgettable

亡 ＋ 心 → 忘

"亡"表示"死亡"，"心"表示"心里"。往事在心中消失了就是"遗忘"。

"亡" means death, "心" means heart. When something ceases to be in your heart you forget it.

| 丶 | 亠 | 亡 | 产 | 忘 | 忘 | 忘 | | | |
|---|---|---|---|---|---|---|---|---|---|

| 忘 | | | | | | | | | |
|---|---|---|---|---|---|---|---|---|---|

85

炎　　　　　yán　scorching

炎热　　yánrè　　　scorching
发炎　　fāyán　　　inflammation
炎症　　yánzhèng　inflammation

火　+　火　→　炎

两个"火"字，一个在下，一个在上，表示火势很大，温度很高。
"火" means fire; and one fire on top of the other depicts a very hot fire.

| 、 | 丷 | 少 | 火 | 炏 | 炏 | 炏 | 炎 | | | |
|---|---|---|---|---|---|---|---|---|---|---|
| 炎 | | | | | | | | | | |

多　　　　　duō　many

很多　　hěnduō　　many
多数　　duōshù　　majority
多少　　duōshǎo　how many

夕　+　夕　→　多

"夕"是古文字"肉"的变体，两块肉重叠在一起，表示数量很多。
"夕" in this case is a variant of "肉" (meat). Two pieces of meat overlapping signify "many, a lot".

| 、 | 夕 | 夕 | 多 | 多 | 多 | | | | | |
|---|---|---|---|---|---|---|---|---|---|---|
| 多 | | | | | | | | | | |

# 光　guāng　light, ray

| | | |
|---|---|---|
| 光明 | guāngmíng | light |
| 阳光 | yángguāng | sunlight |
| 火光 | huǒguāng | flame |

 →  →

古文字中，"光"像一个跪着的人，头上是一个"火"字，表示在黑暗中火给人们带来光明。

The ancient form of "光" resembles a man kneeling down; the upper part "火" (fire) signals fire gives light to people.

| 丨 | 丬 | 屮 | 业 | 光 | 光 | | | | |
|---|---|---|---|---|---|---|---|---|---|

| 光 | | | | | | | | | |
|---|---|---|---|---|---|---|---|---|---|

# 去　qù　go, leave

| | | |
|---|---|---|
| 离去 | líqù | leave |
| 去向 | qùxiàng | the direction |
| 去处 | qùchù | place to go |

 →  →

古代"去"字上部是一个行走的人形，下部的"口"字象征家门口，合在一起表示离家而去。

The upper part of the ancient form of "去" shows a walking man; the lower part depicts an entrance. The two together means leaving home to go somewhere.

| 一 | 十 | 土 | 去 | 去 | | | | | |
|---|---|---|---|---|---|---|---|---|---|

| 去 | | | | | | | | | |
|---|---|---|---|---|---|---|---|---|---|

# 【上下结构(二)】

## TOP – BOTTOM STRUCTURE (2)

上小,下大,书写顺序也是:先上,后下。

Small top, large bottom, order of writing: Top first, then bottom.

灭 [滅]    miè   (of a fire)go out

| | | |
|---|---|---|
| 灭火 | mièhuǒ | put out a fire |
| 消灭 | xiāomiè | perish |
| 灭亡 | mièwáng | be destroyed |

一 ＋ 火 → 灭

"火"是火焰,"一"表示在火上盖压东西,这样,火就可以熄灭了。
"火" means fire, and "一" shows that we use something to cover the fire in order to extinguish it.

| 一 | 一 | 一 | 尹 | 灭 | | |
|---|---|---|---|---|---|---|

| 灭 | | | | | | |
|---|---|---|---|---|---|---|

# 灾 [災]　zāi　disaster, calamity

灾害　zāihài　calamity
火灾　huǒzāi　conflagration
水灾　shuǐzāi　flood

"宀"是一个表示屋顶的偏旁,屋里着火了是一场灾难。

The element "宀" means roof, "火" means fire. If the house goes on fire, it's a disaster.

| 丶 | 宀 | 宀 | 宀 | 宀 | 灾 | 灾 | | | |
|---|---|---|---|---|---|---|---|---|---|
| 灾 | | | | | | | | | |

# 室　shì　room

教室　jiàoshì　classroom
卧室　wòshì　bedroom
室内　shìnèi　indoor

偏旁"宀"表示房屋,"至"是"到"的意思,到房子里边就是"室"。

The element "宀" means roof, "至" means arrive. When we go inside a house, we are in a room.

| 丶 | 宀 | 宀 | 宀 | 室 | 室 | 室 | 室 | 室 | |
|---|---|---|---|---|---|---|---|---|---|
| 室 | | | | | | | | | |

家      jiā   family

| 家庭 | jiātíng | family |
| 家乡 | jiāxiāng | hometown |
| 大家 | dàjiā | everybody |

宀 + 豕 → 家

偏旁"宀"表示房屋，"豕"是猪的意思。在房子周围养猪表示这是一个人家。

The element "宀" indicates a house; "豕" means pig. To have pigs in a house signifies that the house is occupied by a family.

| 丶 | 宀 | 宀 | 宀 | 宁 | 宇 | 宇 | 家 | 家 | 家 |
| 家 | | | | | | | | | |

宝 [寶]      bǎo   treasure

| 宝石 | bǎoshí | precious stone |
| 宝贝 | bǎobèi | treasure |
| 宝贵 | bǎoguì | valuable |

宀 + 玉 → 宝

偏旁"宀"表示房屋，"玉"是玉石，珍贵的东西，家里珍藏的贵重物品。

The element "宀" indicates a house; "玉" means jade, something precious. Something of value in a house is a treasure.

| 丶 | 宀 | 宀 | 宀 | 宁 | 宇 | 宝 | 宝 | | |
| 宝 | | | | | | | | | |

90

# 盲　máng　blind

盲人　mángrén　blind person
盲目　mángmù　blindness
文盲　wénmáng　an illiterate

亡 + 目 → 盲

　　"亡"是死亡的意思，"目"指眼睛，两个字合在一起表示眼睛看不见了。
　　"亡" means to die; "目" means the eyes. The two together mean that one cannot see.

| 、 | 亠 | 亡 | 亠 | 盲 | 盲 | 盲 | 盲 | | |

| 盲 | | | | | | | | | |

# 笔 [筆]　bǐ　pen

毛笔　máobǐ　writing brush
钢笔　gāngbǐ　fountain pen
铅笔　qiānbǐ　pencil

竹 + 毛 → 笔

　　"笔"是由"竹"字演变来的一个偏旁，中国的毛笔，笔杆是用竹子做的，下面是羊或其他动物的毛。
　　"笔" is the bamboo element; "毛" means hair. The handles of Chinese writing brushes are made of bamboo; and the nib is made of hair from animal's like sheep.

| ノ | 丿 | ド | 灶 | 竹 | 竹 | 竺 | 竺 | 竺 | 笔 |

| 笔 | | | | | | | | | |

# 买 [買]　　　mǎi　　buy

| 买主 | mǎizhǔ | buyer |
| 买方 | mǎifāng | the buying part |
| 买价 | mǎijià | buying price |

　　古代"买"字上部的"网"字表示获取，下面的"贝"字表示钱币，用钱换取货物叫"买"。
The upper part of the ancient form of "买" depicts a net "网", which signifies obtaining something. The lower part "贝" (shell) means money. Obtaining something through payment means to buy.

| ⁊ | ⁓ | ⁓ | 㞢 | 买 | 买 | | | | | |
|---|---|---|---|---|---|---|---|---|---|---|
| 买 | | | | | | | | | | |

# 卖 [賣]　　　mài　　sell

| 买卖 | mǎimài | business |
| 卖主 | màizhǔ | seller |
| 卖方 | màifāng | seller |

　　古文字中，"卖"字是在"买"字上加了一个"出"字，表示和"买"相反，是钱进货出。
If we add "出" (go out) above the character "买", we form the character "卖" which signifies the opposite of "买", that is, the goods go out and the money comes in.

| 一 | 十 | 士 | 牛 | 吉 | 志 | 卖 | 卖 | | | |
|---|---|---|---|---|---|---|---|---|---|---|
| 卖 | | | | | | | | | | |

岩　　　　yán　rock
岩石　yánshí　rock
岩洞　yándòng　grotto
岩浆　yánjiāng　magma

山　＋　石　→　岩

"山"上的"石头"是"岩"。

"山" depicts a mountain, and "石" depicts a stone. These two together mean the stones on the mountain, i.e. rocks.

| ⸜ | 山 | 山 | 屵 | 屵 | 岩 | 岩 | 岩 | | |
|---|---|---|---|---|---|---|---|---|---|
| 岩 | | | | | | | | | |

尾　　　　wěi　tail
尾巴　wěibā　tail
结尾　jiéwěi　ending
末尾　mòwěi　end

尸　＋　毛　→　尾

古代"尸"字像人的躯体,在这儿代表动物的躯体,动物的尾巴一般是位于躯体后毛茸茸的。

The ancient form of "尸" resembles a body. Here it represents the body of an animal. "毛" means hair. The animal's tail is found at the back of its body.

| ⸜ | ⸘ | 尸 | 尸 | 尾 | 屋 | 尾 | | | |
|---|---|---|---|---|---|---|---|---|---|
| 尾 | | | | | | | | | |

床　　　chuáng　bed

床单　　chuángdān　　sheet
床位　　chuángwèi　　berth
床头　　chuángtóu　　bedside

广 ＋ 木 → 床

"广"有广大的意思，"木"是木头，"床"是一种较大的木制家具。
"广" means spacious, "木" means wood. "床" is a large piece of wooden furniture.

| 、 | 宀 | 广 | 户 | 斤 | 床 | 床 | | | |
|---|---|---|---|---|---|---|---|---|---|

| 床 | | | | | | | | | |
|---|---|---|---|---|---|---|---|---|---|

系　　　xì　tie, relate to, series

系马　　xìmǎ　　tether a horse
系统　　xìtǒng　　system
系列　　xìliè　　series

丿 ＋ 糸 → 系

"糸"字表示一缕细丝，"丿"一撇表示某物体，两部分合在一起表示在某物体下面悬挂着一缕丝线。
"糸" means a silken thread; "丿" indicates an object. The two together indicate a silken thread hanging from the object.

| 丿 | 乊 | 幺 | 乡 | 幺 | 糸 | 系 | | | |
|---|---|---|---|---|---|---|---|---|---|

| 系 | | | | | | | | | |
|---|---|---|---|---|---|---|---|---|---|

# 【上下结构(三)】

## TOP – BOTTOM STRUCTURE (3)

上大,下小,书写顺序也是:先上,后下。

Large top, small bottom, order of writing: Top first, then bottom.

您    nín    you(respectful)

您好    nínhǎo    how do you do
您早    nínzǎo    good morning

你 + 心 → 您

"你"字是表示第二人称单数的代词,下面加"心"字表示敬称。
"你" is a singular personal pronoun in the 2nd person; and "心" (heart) is added to show respect.

| 亻 | 亻 | 佗 | 竹 | 你 | 你 | 您 | | | |
|---|---|---|---|---|---|---|---|---|---|
| 您 | | | | | | | | | |

黑　　　　hēi　black

| 黑色 | hēisè | black |
| 黑暗 | hēiàn | dark |
| 黑板 | hēibǎn | blackboard |

古代"黑"字上部是"囱"表示烟囱,下面是"炎"字,合在一起表示燃烧后的烟使东西熏黑。

The upper part of the ancient form of "黑" shows a chimney（囱）the lower part "炎" indicates a large fire. The burned places after a fire are black.

| 丶 | 口 | 口 | 口 | 田 | 甲 | 里 | 里 | 黑 | | |
| 黑 | | | | | | | | | | |

墨　　　　mò　China ink

| 墨水 | mòshuǐ | ink |
| 笔墨 | bǐmò | writing |
| 墨镜 | mòjìng | sunglasses |

黑 + 土 → 墨

中国写毛笔字和作画用的"墨"在研磨之前像一种黑色的土。

In China ink is used in painting and calligraphy. Before it is mixed with water for use, it is a solid mass like a moulded lump of black earth.

| 黑 | 墨 | | | | | | | |
| 墨 | | | | | | | | |

建      jiàn    establish, build

建设 jiànshè construct
建立 jiànlì establish
建议 jiànyì propose

聿 ＋ 廴 → 建

古代"聿"字表示执笔,"廴"字旁表示延长。把事物记载下来,使其长期保留,叫"建立"档案。

The ancient form of "聿" shows a hand with a brush writing something down, "廴" means to prolong. Writing something down to keep it for a long time is to "establish" as an archive.

| ⁊ | ⁊ | ⁊ | ⁊ | ⁊ | 聿 | 建 | 建 | | | |
|---|---|---|---|---|---|---|---|---|---|---|

| 建 | | | | | | | | | | |
|---|---|---|---|---|---|---|---|---|---|---|

丝 [絲]      sī    silk

丝绸 sīchóu silk cloth
丝线 sīxiàn silk thread
肉丝 ròusī shredded meat

絲 → 絲 → 絲 → 丝

古代"糸"字像一缕绞着的细丝,两个"糸"字表示很多细丝在一起。

The ancient form of "糸" depicts twisted silken threads; and two silken threads imply many silken threads.

| ⼁ | ⼁ | 丝 | 丝 | 丝 | | | | | | |
|---|---|---|---|---|---|---|---|---|---|---|

| 丝 | | | | | | | | | | |
|---|---|---|---|---|---|---|---|---|---|---|

# 【内外结构】

## IN – OUT STRUCTURE

内外结构,书写顺序是:先外,后内,最后封口。

Order of writing: Outside first, then inside, finally close by drawing the bottom.

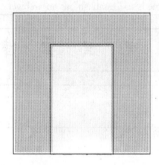

| 内 | nèi   inner, inside | 内部 | nèibù | interior |
|---|---|---|---|---|
| | | 内科 | nèikē | internal medicine |
| | | 内容 | nèiróng | content |

门 + 入 → 内

"门"表示一定的范围,"入"字表示进入,进入里边是"内"。

"门" indicates a certain limit; "入" means to "enter". The two together signify "inside".

| 丨 | 冂 | 内 | 内 | | | | | | |
|---|---|---|---|---|---|---|---|---|---|
| 内 | | | | | | | | | |

同　　tóng　same, in common

| 同样 | tóngyàng | same |
| 同意 | tóngyì | agree |
| 同学 | tóngxué | schoolmate |

冂 ＋ 一 ＋ 口 → 同

　　　"冂"字表示一定的范围,"口"表示说话,某些人说的话一样,像出自一人之口。

"冂" indicates a certain limit; "口" means speaking. When several people are saying the same words one after another, it is as though only one person was speaking.

| 丨 | 冂 | 冂 | 同 | 同 | 同 | | | | |

| 同 | | | | | | | | | |

国 [國]　　guó　country

| 国家 | guójiā | country |
| 中国 | zhōngguó | China |
| 国际 | guójì | international |

口 ＋ 或 ＋ 國 → 国

　　　古代"或"字表示用武器守卫的地方,外边加一个"口"表示疆界,合在一起就是国家的意思。

The ancient form of "或" depicts a place defended by armed forces; "口" stands for the borders. Putting the two parts together means country.

| 丨 | 冂 | 冂 | 冃 | 用 | 国 | 国 | 国 | | |

| 国 | | | | | | | | | |

# COMBINED CHARACTERS（2）— PICTOPHONOGRAMS

### 形声字

　　形声字也是一种合体字。构成合体字的两部分,一部分表意和字的意义有关,另一部分表音和字的读音有关,这种合体字叫形声字。表意的偏旁叫作"形旁",表音的偏旁叫作"声旁"。如:

| 女 | + | 马 | → | 妈 |
| nǚ woman | | mǎ horse | | mā mother |
| 形旁 | | 声旁 | | 形声字 |
| signific | | phonetic | | pictophonogram |

　　"妈"是女性,所以用"女"字旁,"马"表示"妈"字的读音。

　　形声字占汉字的总数的80%以上,数量最多,但如果你掌握了独体字,学习形声字并不困难。因为构成形声字"形旁"的,有的就是一个独体字,有的是由独体字演变来的符号;"声旁"一般是一个独体字或一个合体字。

　　形声字的"形旁"的作用是表示意义的类别,因此,了解一个字的"形旁"可以帮助人们掌握和记忆字形和字义。

　　在学习形声字时要注意是:由于语言的演变和文字的不同步性,它们的声旁,有的和字音相同,但多数是不完全相同的,所以学习形声字,对有的字可以借助"声旁"来记发音,对大多数字还要通过拼音来掌握字音。

### Pictophonograms

　　Among the combined characters there is one kind which is composed of a part indicating its meaning and the other indicating its pronunciation. The first part is called the "signific" and the second the "phonetic". Characters of this kind are called "pictophonogram". e.g.

　　A mother is female, so the "女" (woman) component is used. "马" indicates the pronunciation of "妈".

　　Pictophonograms account for more than 80% of all Chinese characters. Although their number is quite big, they are not too hard to learn when one is familiar with the independent characters because the signific in many case is an independent character and in others a variant derived from an independent character. The phonetic is usually an independent or a combined character. When the independent characters are mastered, the pictophonograms are easy to learn.

　　The signific of a pictophonogram is supposed to indicate the domain to which the pictophonogram's meaning is related. Therefore, understanding a pictophonogram's signific helps to learn and memorize it.

　　When you learn the pictophonograms, you should pay attention to the development of the spoken language, there may be cases where the phonetic indicates a pictophonogram's pronunciation faithfully, but in many cases it doesn't represent the exact pronunciation of the pictophonogram. So knowing the pronunciation of the phonetic sometimes helps but in very many cases it does not. You should use Pinyin to remember the pronunciation of most pictophonograms.

住      zhù    dwell, live

| 住址 | zhùzhǐ | address |
| 住房 | zhùfáng | housing |
| 居住 | jūzhù | reside |

亻   +   主   →   住

"亻"是"人"字的变体，作形旁；"主"[zhǔ]是声旁。"住"是"人"的活动。

"亻" is a variant of "人" and acts as a signific. "主" is the phonetic. Dwelling is an action of "人", that is, of people.

| 丿 | 亻 | 亻 | 亻 | 住 | 住 | 住 | | | |
|---|---|---|---|---|---|---|---|---|---|
| 住 | | | | | | | | | |

剪      jiǎn    scissors, cut, clip

| 剪子 | jiǎnzi | scissors |
| 剪刀 | jiǎndāo | scissors |
| 剪裁 | jiǎncái | cut out, tailor |

前   +   刀   →   剪

"前"[qián]是声旁，"刀"作形旁。剪子是由两把"刀"构成的。

"前"(qián) is the phonetic while "刀"(knife) is the signific. The scissors are composed of two knires.

| 丶 | 丷 | 丷 | 广 | 艹 | 首 | 首 | 前 | 前 | 剪 | 剪 |
|---|---|---|---|---|---|---|---|---|---|---|
| 剪 | | | | | | | | | | |

勇　　　yǒng　brave

勇敢　yǒnggǎn　brave
勇气　yǒngqì　courage
勇士　yǒngshì　warrior

甬 ＋ 力 → 勇

"甬"[yǒng]是声旁,"力"作形旁。有力气的人往往表现得很"勇敢"。
"甬"(yǒng) is the phonetic and "力"(strength) is the signific. A person of strength will usually be brave.

| ⁊ | ⁊ | ⁊ | 圅 | 圅 | 甬 | 甬 | 勇 | 勇 | | |
|---|---|---|---|---|---|---|---|---|---|---|
| 勇 | | | | | | | | | | |

冻 [凍]　dòng　freeze

冻结　dòngjié　congeal
冻死　dòngsǐ　freeze to death
冻冰　dòngbīng　freeze

冫 ＋ 东 → 冻

"冫"是形旁,表示寒冷;"东"[dōng]作声旁。由于寒冷才使人或东西受"冻"。
The signific "冫" means cold, "东" is the phonetic. In cold temperatures people and things will freeze.

| 、 | 冫 | 仒 | 냐 | 冻 | 冻 | 冻 | | | | |
|---|---|---|---|---|---|---|---|---|---|---|
| 冻 | | | | | | | | | | |

102

邮 [郵]　　yóu　　post, mail

邮局　　yóujú　　post office
邮票　　yóupiào　　stamp
集邮　　jíyóu　　to collect stamps

由 ＋ 阝 → 邮

"由"[yóu] 是声旁；"阝"是形旁,表示城邑。信件从一个地区传送到另一个地区叫"邮寄"。

"由" is the phonetic. The significant "阝" means a city-state. Letters are sent from one city to another by mail.

| 丶 | 冂 | 日 | 由 | 由 | 由阝 | 邮 | | | |
|---|---|---|---|---|---|---|---|---|---|
| 邮 | | | | | | | | | |

城　　chéng　　city wall, city

城市　　chénshì　　town, city
长城　　Chángchén　　the Great Wall
城里　　chénlǐ　　in town

土 ＋ 成 → 城

"土"是形旁,"成"[chéng] 作声旁。城墙是由"土"修筑成的。

"土" (soil) is the significant. "成" is the phonetic. In ancient times city walls were made of earth.

| 土 | 圵 | 圹 | 圻 | 城 | 城 | 城 | | | |
|---|---|---|---|---|---|---|---|---|---|
| 城 | | | | | | | | | |

巧　　qiǎo　clever, skilful

| 巧妙 | qiǎomiào | ingenious |
| 巧干 | qiǎogàn | work ingeniously |
| 灵巧 | língqiǎo | dexterous |

工 ＋ 丂 → 巧

　　　　"工"是形旁，"丂"作声旁。能用手作很精细的活儿称之为手"巧"。
"工"（work）is the signific and "丂" is the phonetic. One who can work with his hands on fine things is said to be skilful.

| 工 | 工 | 巧 | | | | | | | |
|---|---|---|---|---|---|---|---|---|---|

| 巧 | | | | | | | | | |
|---|---|---|---|---|---|---|---|---|---|

唱　　chàng　sing

| 唱歌 | chànggē | sing(a song) |
| 唱片 | chàngpiàn | disc |
| 合唱 | héchàng | chorus |

口 ＋ 昌 → 唱

　　　　"口"是形旁，"昌"[chāng] 是声旁。"唱歌"是"口腔"的动作。
"口"（mouth）is the signific and "昌" is the phonetic. Singing is an action of the mouth.

|丨| 口 | 口 | 口丨 | 口冂 | 口日 | 吧 | 唱 | 唱 | 唱 |
|---|---|---|---|---|---|---|---|---|---|

| 唱 | | | | | | | | | |
|---|---|---|---|---|---|---|---|---|---|

园 [園]　　**yuán**　**garden**

公园　　gōngyuán　park
花园　　huāyuán　garden
园林　　yuánlín　gardens

口　＋　元　→　园

　　"口"是形旁,表示一定的界限,"元"[ yuán ]是声旁。"园子"是用某些东西圈起的地方。
The signific"口" indicates a certain limit, "元" is the phonetic. A garden is a place enclosed by something.

| 丨 | 冂 | 冂 | 冃 | 冄 | 园 | 园 | | | |
|---|---|---|---|---|---|---|---|---|---|
| 园 | | | | | | | | | |

帽　　　**mào**　**headgear**

帽子　　màozi　headgear
草帽　　cǎomào　straw hat
礼帽　　lǐmào　top hat

巾　＋　冒　→　帽

　　"巾"是形旁,"冒"[ mào ]是声旁。"帽子"的作用像把"头巾"围在头上一样。
"巾"（towel）is the signific and "冒" is the phonetic. In China, a common type of headgear is a towel worn like a turban.

| 丨 | 冂 | 巾 | 巾 | 巾 | 巾 | 帽 | 帽 | 帽 | 帽 |
|---|---|---|---|---|---|---|---|---|---|
| 帽 | | | | | | | | | |

岭　　**lǐng　mountain range**

山岭　　shānlǐng　mountain
岭南　　Lǐng'nán　Ling'nan
秦岭　　Qínlǐng　Qin Ridges

山 ＋ 令 → 岭

"山"是形旁,"令"[ lǐng ]是声旁。"岭"的意思指"山脉"。

"山"(mountain) is the signific and "令" is the phonetic. "岭" means mountain range.

| 丨 | 山 | 山 | 山 | 屵 | 屵 | 岭 | 岭 | | |

| 岭 | | | | | | | | | |

彩　　**cǎi　colour**

彩色　　cǎisè　multicolour
色彩　　sècǎi　colour
光彩　　guāngcǎi lustre

采 ＋ 彡 → 彩

"采"[ cǎi ]是声旁,"彡"是形旁,表示四射的光芒。

"采" is the phonetic. The signific "彡" shows rays of light.

| ′ | ′ | ′′ | ′′ | 平 | 平 | 采 | 采 | 彩 | 彩 | 彩 |

| 彩 | | | | | | | | | | |

106

庭　　tíng　front courtyard

| 家庭 | jiātíng | family |
| 法庭 | fǎtíng | tribunal |
| 庭院 | tíngyuàn | courtyard |

广 ＋ 廷 → 庭

"广"是形旁,表示和房屋有关,"廷"[tíng]作声旁。"庭"本义指厅堂。

The signific "广" refers to a house, "廷" is the phonetic. "庭" originally means the front courtyard of a house.

| 广 | 广 | 庀 | 庄 | 庄 | 庭 | 庭 | | | |

| 庭 | | | | | | | | | |

---

厅 [廳]　　tīng　hall

| 客厅 | kètīng | drawing room |
| 餐厅 | cāntīng | dining hall |
| 饭厅 | fàntīng | dining room |

厂 ＋ 丁 → 厅

"厂"是"广"的简体,作形旁,"丁"[dīng]作声旁。"客厅"是接待客人的房间。

The signific "厂" is a simplification of "广". "丁" is the phonetic. The parlour is a room to receive guests in.

| 一 | 厂 | 厂 | 厅 | | | | | | |

| 厅 | | | | | | | | | |

问 [問]　**wèn**　ask, interrogate

| 问题 | wèntí | question |
| 提问 | tíwèn | ask |
| 疑问 | yíwèn | query |

门 ＋ 口 → 问

"门"[ mén ] 是声旁,"口"作形旁。用"口"来"询问"。

"门" is the phonetic. "口" (mouth) is the signific. One has to open the mouth when asking a question.

| 丶 | 冂 | 冂 | 冋 | 问 | 问 | | | | |
|---|---|---|---|---|---|---|---|---|---|

| 问 | | | | | | | | | |
|---|---|---|---|---|---|---|---|---|---|

客　**kè**　visitor

| 客人 | kèrén | visitor |
| 请客 | qǐngkè | stand treat |
| 会客 | huìkè | receive a visitor |

宀 ＋ 各 → 客

"宀"是形旁,表示人居住的房屋,"各"[ gè ] 作声旁。到家里的人称为"客人"。

The signific "宀" indicates a roof of a house. "各" is the phonetic. People who come under one's roof are guests.

| 丶 | 丷 | 宀 | 宁 | 岁 | 灾 | 灾 | 客 | 客 | |
|---|---|---|---|---|---|---|---|---|---|

| 客 | | | | | | | | | |
|---|---|---|---|---|---|---|---|---|---|

屁     pì   fart

| 放屁 | fàngpì | break wind |
| 屁股 | pìgu | bottom |
| 屁话 | pìhuà | shit |

尸 ＋ 比 → 屁

"尸"是形旁,表示和人体有关,"比"[ bǐ ] 作声旁。"屁"是"人体"排出的气体。

The signific "尸" shows that word has to do with the human body. "比" is the phonetic. "屁" refers to the air emitted from the human body.

| 尸 | 尸 | 尼 | 屁 | 屁 | | | | | |
|---|---|---|---|---|---|---|---|---|---|

| 屁 | | | | | | | | | |
|---|---|---|---|---|---|---|---|---|---|

张 [張] zhāng   draw, open, spread

| 张开 | zhāngkāi | open |
| 张口 | zhāngkǒu | open the mouth |
| 夸张 | kuāzhāng | exaggerate |

弓 ＋ 长 → 张

"弓"是形旁,"长"[ zhāng ] 作声旁。"弓"有"张",有"弛"。

"弓" is the signific and "长" is the phonetic. A bow can be drawn and relased.

| ㇇ | ㇉ | 弓 | 弓' | 弘 | 张 | 张 | | | |
|---|---|---|---|---|---|---|---|---|---|

| 张 | | | | | | | | | |
|---|---|---|---|---|---|---|---|---|---|

婚　　　hūn　marry

| 结婚 | jiéhūn | marry |
| 离婚 | líhūn | divorce |
| 婚礼 | hūnlǐ | wedding |

女　+　昏　→　婚

"女"是形旁，"昏"[ hūn ]作声旁。"结婚"和"女子"有关。

"女" is the signific and "昏" is the phonetic. Getting married and marriage of course have to do with woman.

| 〈 | 〈 | 女 | 女′ | 女丨 | 女丨 | 妡 | 妡 | 娇 | 婚 | 婚 |

| 婚 | | | | | | | | | | |

孩　　　hái　child

| 孩子 | háizi | child |
| 小孩 | xiǎohái | child |
| 男孩 | nánhái | boy |

子　+　亥　→　孩

"子"是形旁，表示孩子，"亥"[ hài ]作声旁。

The signific "子" means a child and "亥" is the phonetic.

| ⁻ | 了 | 子 | 孑 | 孑′ | 孑亠 | 孩 | 孩 | 孩 | | |

| 孩 | | | | | | | | | | |

110

# 骑 [騎] qí ride(an animal)

骑马   qí mǎ   ride a horse
骑车   qí chē   by bicycle
骑士   qíshì   knight

马 + 奇 → 骑

"马"是形旁，"奇"作［qí］声旁。人在"马"上叫"骑"。

"马" is the signific and "奇" is the phonetic. What people do on horseback is "to ride"（骑）.

| ㇆ | 马 | 马 | 马 | 马 | 马 | 骑 | 骑 | 骑 | 骑 |

| 骑 | | | | | | | | | |

# 草 cǎo grass, straw

草地   cǎodì   grassland
青草   qīngcǎo   green grass
花草   huācǎo   flowers and plants

"艹"是形旁，古代是个象形字，表示"草"，"早"［zǎo］作声旁。

In ancient times the signific "艹" was a pictogram that looked like grass. "早" is the phonetic.

| 一 | 十 | 艹 | 艻 | 节 | 苔 | 苩 | 苴 | 草 | |

| 草 | | | | | | | | | |

# 线 [綫]　xiàn　thread, line

毛线　máoxiàn　knitting wool
电线　diànxian　electric wire
光线　guāngxiàn　ray

纟　+　戋　→　线

"纟"是形旁,表示和丝线有关,"戋"[ jiàn ] 作声旁。

The "纟" is the significant and indicates that the word has to do with threads of silk. "戋" is the phonetic.

| ⺈ | 纟 | 纟 | 纟 | 纟 | 线 | 线 | 线 | | | |
|---|---|---|---|---|---|---|---|---|---|---|

| 线 | | | | | | | | | | |
|---|---|---|---|---|---|---|---|---|---|---|

# 近　jìn　near

近来　jìnlái　recently
近代　jìndài　modern times
近道　jìdào　shortcut

辶　+　斤　→　近

"辶"是形旁,表示和行走有关,"斤"[ jīn ] 作声旁。距离远近和行走有关。

The significant "辶" indicates that the word has to do with walking. "斤" is the phonetic. Whether something is near or far relates to walking.

| ⺀ | 厂 | 斤 | 斤 | 近 | 近 | 近 | | | | |
|---|---|---|---|---|---|---|---|---|---|---|

| 近 | | | | | | | | | | |
|---|---|---|---|---|---|---|---|---|---|---|

112

理　　lǐ　texture, reason

| 理发 | lǐfà | haircut |
| 理论 | lǐlùn | theory |
| 经理 | jīnglǐ | manager |

王 ＋ 里 → 理

"王"是形旁，在这个字里代表"玉"，"里"［lǐ］作声旁。"玉石"是有"纹理"的。

Here the signific "王" is a viriant of "玉" (jade). "里" is the phonetic. Jade has a certain texture.

| 一 | 二 | 干 | 王 | 玙 | 玗 | 玾 | 玾 | 玾 | 理 | 理 |

| 理 | | | | | | | | | | |

机 [機]　　jī　machine

| 飞机 | fēijī | plane |
| 机场 | jīchǎng | airport |
| 机器 | jīqì | machine |

木 ＋ 几 → 机

"木"是形旁，"几"［jī］作声旁。中国过去的"机器"是"木"制的。

"木" is the signific and "几" is the phonetic. In the old days all machines were made of wood.

| 一 | 十 | 扌 | 木 | 朾 | 机 | | | | |

| 机 | | | | | | | | | |

猫　　　　　māo　cat

| 小猫 | xiǎomāo | kitten |
|------|---------|--------|
| 熊猫 | xióngmāo | panda |
| 猫叫 | māojiào | mewing |

犭 ＋ 苗 → 猫

"犭"是形旁，表示和兽类有关，"苗"[ miáo ] 作声旁。"猫"是一种动物。
The significic "犭" shows that the word has to do with animal. "苗" is the phonetic. Cat is an animal.

| ⺁ | ⺁ | 犭 | 犭 | 犲 | 犲 | 猫 | 猫 | 猫 | 猫 |
|---|---|---|---|---|---|---|---|---|---|

| 猫 | | | | | | | | | |
|---|---|---|---|---|---|---|---|---|---|

轮 [輪]　　　　lún　wheel

| 轮子 | lúnzi | wheel |
|------|-------|-------|
| 轮船 | lúnchuán | steamer |
| 车轮 | chēlún | wheel |

车 ＋ 仑 → 轮

"车"是形旁，"仑"[ lún ] 作声旁。"轮子"是"车"的一部分。
"车" is the significic and "仑" is the phonetic. Wheel is a part of a vehicle.

| 一 | 𠂉 | 车 | 车 | 轮 | 轮 | 轮 | | | |
|---|---|---|---|---|---|---|---|---|---|

| 轮 | | | | | | | | | |
|---|---|---|---|---|---|---|---|---|---|

# 战 [戰]　　zhàn　fight, war

| 战争 | zhànzhēng | war |
| 战士 | zhànshì | soldier |
| 战斗 | zhàndòu | fight |

占 ＋ 戈 → 战

"占"[zhàn] 是声旁，"戈"是一种兵器，在这个字里作形旁，表示和兵器有关。"作战"要用兵器。
"占" is the phonetic. The signific "戈" originated as a pictogram refers to a weapon. Arms like that are used when one goes to war.

| 丨 | 卜 | 上 | 占 | 占 | 占 | 战 | 战 | 战 | | |

| 战 | | | | | | | | | | |

# 放　　fàng　put, let go, let off

| 摆放 | bǎifàng | put |
| 解放 | jiěfàng | liberate |
| 开放 | kāifàng | open |

方 ＋ 攵 → 放

"方"[fɑng] 是声旁，"攵"是形旁，表示和手的动作有关。"放"东西是要用手的。
"方" is the phonetic. "攵" is the signific and indicates that the word has to do with an action of the hand. Things are put in some place by hands.

| 丶 | 亠 | 亍 | 方 | 方 | 放 | 放 | 放 | | | |

| 放 | | | | | | | | | | |

115

晨　　　chén　morning

日 ＋ 辰 → 晨

"日"是形旁，"辰"[ chén ]作声旁。太阳刚升起的时候叫"早晨"。

"日" is the significant and "辰" is the phonetic. The moment when the sun is rising is morning.

丶　丨　冂　冃　日　旦　旻　昃　昃　晨　晨　晨

晨

财 [財]　cái　wealth, money

贝 ＋ 才 → 财

"贝"是形旁，表示和钱财有关，"才"[ cái ]作声旁。

"贝" is the significant and indicates the word has to do with money. "才" is the phonetic.

丨　冂　贝　贝　贝一　财　财

财

116

# 视 [視]　　shì　look at

视力　　shìlì　　sight
电视　　diànshì　television
重视　　zhòngshì　pay attention to

礻 ＋ 见 → 视

"礻"是"示"[ shì ]字的变体，在这个字里作声旁，"见"作形旁。"视"是观看的意思。
The phonetic "礻" is a variant of "示". "见" is the signific. "视" means "to look at".

| 丶 | ㇇ | ㇈ | 礻 | 礻 | 礽 | 视 | 视 | | | |
|---|---|---|---|---|---|---|---|---|---|---|

| 视 | | | | | | | | | | |
|---|---|---|---|---|---|---|---|---|---|---|

# 犁　　lí　phouhg

犁头　　lítou　plough
犁地　　lídì　to plough
犁田　　lítián　to plough

利 ＋ 牛 → 犁

"利"[ lì ]是声旁，"牛"作形旁。"犁"是要用"牛"拉的。
"利" is the phonetic. and"牛" (ox) is the signific. The plough is drawn by the ox.

| ノ | 二 | 千 | 禾 | 禾 | 利 | 利 | 利 | 利 | 型 | 犁 |
|---|---|---|---|---|---|---|---|---|---|---|

| 犁 | | | | | | | | | | |
|---|---|---|---|---|---|---|---|---|---|---|

指       zhǐ   finger

手指   shǒuzhǐ   finger
指导   zhǐdǎo   guide
指挥   zhǐhuī   command

扌 + 旨 → 指

"扌"是"手"字的变体,"旨"[ zhǐ ]作声旁。"手指"是"手"的一部分。

The signific "扌" is a variant of "手" (hand) and "旨" is the phonetic. A finger is a part of the hand.

| 一 | 扌 | 扌 | 扩 | 拃 | 拃 | 指 | 指 | 指 | | |

| 指 | | | | | | | | | | |

爬       pá   crawl, climb

爬山   páshān   climb a mountain
爬行   páxíng   crawl
爬虫   páchóng   reptile

爪 + 巴 → 爬

"爪"是形旁,"巴"[ bā ]作声旁。动物在地上"爬行"是要用"爪子"的。

"爪" (claw) is the signific and "巴" is the phonetic. Some animals use their claws to crawl on the ground.

| 丿 | 厂 | 爪 | 爪 | 爪 | 爬 | 爬 | 爬 | | | |

| 爬 | | | | | | | | | | |

118

# 爸　bà　father

爸爸　　bàba　　papa, dad

"父"是形旁，"巴"[ bā ]作声旁。"父亲"又叫"爸爸"。

"父" (father) is the significant and "巴" is the phonetic. A father may be addressed "爸爸" by his children.

| ′ | ハ | ゲ | 父 | 爷 | 爷 | 谷 | 爸 | | | |
|---|---|---|---|---|---|---|---|---|---|---|

| 爸 | | | | | | | | | | |
|---|---|---|---|---|---|---|---|---|---|---|

# 斧　fǔ　axe, hatchet

斧子　　fǔzi　　axe
斧头　　fǔtóu　　axe
斧正　　fǔzhèng　make correction

$$父 + 斤 → 斧$$

"父"[ fù ] 是声旁，"斤"作形旁，表示和砍折有关。"斧子"是一种砍伐的工具。

"父" is the phonetic. The significant "斤" indicates that the word has to do with cutting or felling trees. An axe is a tool to cut or fell trees.

| ′ | ハ | ゲ | 父 | 父 | 斧 | 斧 | 斧 | | | |
|---|---|---|---|---|---|---|---|---|---|---|

| 斧 | | | | | | | | | | |
|---|---|---|---|---|---|---|---|---|---|---|

期　　　qī　a period of time

日期　　riqī　date
时期　　shíqī　period
学期　　xuéqī　school term

其　＋　月　→　期

"其" [ qí ] 是声旁，"月"是"日月"的"月"，在这儿作形旁，表示和日期有关。

"其" is the phonetic. The signific "月" (moon) indicates that the word has to do with date and time.

| 一 | 广 | 卄 | 甘 | 甘 | 其 | 其 | 其 | 期 | | | |
|---|---|---|---|---|---|---|---|---|---|---|---|
| 期 | | | | | | | | | | | |

肚　　　dù　belly

肚子　　dùzi　belly
肚脐　　dùqí　navel
肚皮　　dùpí　belly

月　＋　土　→　肚

这个"月"是从"肉"字演变来的，作形旁，"土" [tǔ] 是声旁。"肚子"是人肉体的一部分。

This signific "月" is a variant of "肉" (meat). "土" is the phonetic. The belly is a part of the body.

| 丿 | 刀 | 月 | 月 | 月 | 肚 | 肚 | | | | |
|---|---|---|---|---|---|---|---|---|---|---|
| 肚 | | | | | | | | | | |

歌　　　　　gē　song

唱歌　chànggē　sing
歌曲　gēqǔ　song
民歌　míngē　folk song

哥 ＋ 欠 → 歌

　　"哥"[ ge ] 是声旁，"欠"是形旁，表示和嘴出气有关。"歌"是口中唱出来的。
"哥" is the phonetic. The signific "欠" indicates that the word has to do with the air coming from the mouth. A song comes out of the mouth, too.

| 一 | 一 | 一 | 一 | 可 | 可 | 哥 | 哥 | 歌 | | |

| 歌 | | | | | | | | | | |

烟　　　yān　smoke, tabacco

烟火　yānhuǒ　smoke and fire
香烟　xiāngyān　cigarette
吸烟　xīyān　to smoke

火 ＋ 因 → 烟

　　"火"是形旁，"因"[ yīn ] 作声旁。"烟"是由"火"产生的。
"火" is the signific and "因" is the phonetic. Smoke comes from fire.

| 丶 | 丷 | 少 | 火 | 灯 | 灯 | 炉 | 烔 | 烟 | 烟 |

| 烟 | | | | | | | | | |

照　zhào　shine, illuminate

照明　zhàomíng　lighting
照相　zhàoxiàng　to photograph
照片　zhàopiàn　photograph

昭　+　灬　→　照

"昭"[ zhāo ]是声旁,"灬"是"火"字的变体,作形旁。"火光"可以"照明"。

"昭" is the phonetic. The signific " 灬 " is a variant of "火" (fire). Fire gives light.

| 丨 | 冂 | 冃 | 日 | 日⁷ | 昭 | 昭 | 昭 | 昭 | 照 | |
|---|---|---|---|---|---|---|---|---|---|---|

| 照 | | | | | | | | | | |

房　fáng　house

房子　fángzi　house
房间　fángjiān　room
楼房　lóufáng　building

户　+　方　→　房

"户"是形旁,"方"[ fāng ]作声旁。"门"是"房子"的重要组成部分。

"户" (door) is the signific and "方" is the phonetic. Door is an important part of a house.

| 、 | 丶⁷ | 冫 | 户 | 户 | 户 | 启 | 房 | | | |
|---|---|---|---|---|---|---|---|---|---|---|

| 房 | | | | | | | | | | |

# 想

**xiǎng  think**

思想　　sīxiǎng　　thought
想法　　xiǎngfǎ　　idea, opinion
理想　　lǐxiǎng　　ideal

相 ＋ 心 → 想

　　"相"[xiàng]是声旁,"心"作形旁,表示和心里活动有关。"想"是一种心里活动。
"想" is the phonetic. The signific "心" indicates something taking place in one's heart. Thinking "想" is commonly thought of as having its seat in the heart.

| 一 | 十 | 才 | 木 | 相 | 相 | 想 | 想 | 想 | | |
|---|---|---|---|---|---|---|---|---|---|---|
| 想 | | | | | | | | | | |

# 情

**qíng  feeling, affection**

感情　　gǎnqíng　　emotion
爱情　　àiqíng　　love
情况　　qíngkuàng　　situation

忄 ＋ 青 → 情

　　"忄"是"心"字的变体,作形旁,"青"[qīng]是声旁。"情感"是一种心里活动。
The signific "忄" is a variant of "心" (heart). "青" is the phonetic. Feelings are popularly thought of as activities of the heart.

| 丶 | 丬 | 忄 | 忄一 | 忄二 | 忄主 | 性 | 情 | 情 | 情 | 情 |
|---|---|---|---|---|---|---|---|---|---|---|
| 情 | | | | | | | | | | |

汞　**gǒng　mercury**

| | | |
|---|---|---|
| 汞物 | gǒngwù | mercuride |
| 汞化 | gǒnghuà | mercuration |
| 汞柱 | gǒngzhù | mercury column |

工　+　水　→　汞

　　　"工"〔gōng〕是声旁，"水"是形旁，表示和水或液体有关。"汞"是一种液体。
"工" is the phonetic. The signific "水" indicates that the word has to do with liquids. Mercury is a liquid substance.

| 一 | 丆 | 工 | 于 | 严 | 乥 | 汞 | | | |
|---|---|---|---|---|---|---|---|---|---|

| 汞 | | | | | | | | | |
|---|---|---|---|---|---|---|---|---|---|

河　**hé　river**

| | | |
|---|---|---|
| 黄河 | Huánghé | the Yellow River |
| 山河 | shānhé | territory |
| 河北 | Héběi | Hebei(province) |

氵　+　可　→　河

　　　"氵"是"水"的变体，作形旁，"可"〔kě〕是声旁。"水"流成"河"
The signific "氵" is a variant of "水" (water) "可" is the phonetic. Running water forms a river.

| 丶 | 冫 | 氵 | 氵 | 沪 | 沪 | 沪 | 河 | | |
|---|---|---|---|---|---|---|---|---|---|

| 河 | | | | | | | | | |
|---|---|---|---|---|---|---|---|---|---|

124

神　　shén　god, deity

| 鬼神 | guǐshén | gods and spirit |
| 精神 | jīngshen | spirit |
| 神气 | shénqì | expression |

礻 ＋ 申 → 神

"礻"是"示"字的变体,作形旁表示和祭祀、鬼神有关。"申"[ shēn ]作声旁。

The significant "礻" is a variant of "示" and indicates that the word has to do with sacrifices, ghosts and gods. "申" is the phonetic.

| 礻 | 礻 | 和 | 和 | 袖 | 神 | | | | |
|---|---|---|---|---|---|---|---|---|---|

| 神 | | | | | | | | | |
|---|---|---|---|---|---|---|---|---|---|

矿 [礦]　　kuàng　ore, mine

| 矿石 | kuàngshí | ore |
| 矿山 | kuàngshān | mine |
| 煤矿 | méikuàng | coal mine |

石 ＋ 广 → 矿

"石"是形旁,"广"[ guǎng ]作声旁。"矿"是富有开采价值的"石头"。

"石"(stone) is the significant. "广" is the phonetic. The ore is a type of stone containing valuable minerals and may be mined.

| 一 | 丆 | 丆 | 石 | 石 | 矿 | 矿 | 矿 | | |
|---|---|---|---|---|---|---|---|---|---|

| 矿 | | | | | | | | | |
|---|---|---|---|---|---|---|---|---|---|

125

眠　　　mián　sleep

| 睡眠 | shuìmián | sleep |
| 安眠 | ānmián | sleep peacefully |
| 冬眠 | dōngmián | hibernate |

目 ＋ 民 → 眠

"目"是形旁，"民"[ mín ]作声旁。"睡眠"时，"眼睛"要闭上。

"目"（eye）is the signific. "民" is the phonetic. The eyes are closed when one sleeps.

| 丨 | 冂 | 冃 | 月 | 目 | 目ˊ | 目ˋ | 眂 | 眠 | 眠 |

| 眠 | | | | | | | | | |

界　　　jiè　scope, boundary

| 世界 | shìjiè | world |
| 国界 | guójiè | national boundary |
| 界限 | jièxiàn | limits |

田 ＋ 介 → 界

"田"是形旁，"介"[ jiè ]是声旁。"田地"是有"边界"的。

"田"（field）is the signific. "介" is the phonetic. A field has a definite boundary.

| 丶 | 冂 | 囗 | 田 | 田 | 罘 | 界 | 界 | 界 |

| 界 | | | | | | | | |

126

盛　　chéng　　fill, ladle, hold

| 盛饭 | chéng fàn | fill a bowl with rice |
| 盛菜 | chéng cài | ladle food |
| 盛器 | chéngqì | vessel |

成 ＋ 皿 → 盛

　　"成"［chéng］是声旁，"皿"是古代盛物的器具，作形旁。把东西放在器皿里叫"盛"。
"成" is the phonetic. "皿" is a pictogram for household utensils and serves as the significant. Putting things into a household container is to fill.

| 一 | 厂 | 厉 | 成 | 成 | 成 | 成 | 盛 | 盛 | 盛 | 盛 |

| 盛 | | | | | | | | | | |

种　　zhòng　　grow, plant, sow

| 种地 | zhòng dì | till the fields |
| 种花 | zhòng huā | grow flowers |
| 种田 | zhòng tián | till the paddy fields |

禾 ＋ 中 → 种

　　"禾"是形旁，表示和庄稼有关，"中"［zhōng］作声旁。"禾苗"是"种"出来的。
The significant "禾" (seedling) indicates that the word has to do with crops. "中" is the phonetic. Seedlings appear only after one has sown.

| ノ | 二 | 千 | 禾 | 禾 | 禾 | 和 | 和 | 种 |

| 种 | | | | | | | | |

病　bìng　ill, sick, disease

病人　bìngrén　patient
病情　bìngqíng　state of an illness
生病　shēngbìng　fall ill

疒 ＋ 丙 → 病

"疒"是形旁，表示和疾病有关，"丙"[ bǐng ] 作声旁。
The signific "疒" indicates that the word has to do with illness. "丙" is the phonetic.

丶　亠　广　广　疒　疒　疒　病　病　病

病

站　zhàn　stand, station

站立　zhànlì　stand
车站　chēzhàn　station
站住　zhànzhù　stop

立 ＋ 占 → 站

"立"是形旁，"占"[ zhàn ] 作声旁。"站"和"立"是同义词。
"立"(stand) is the signific and "占"is the phonetic. "站" and "立" both mean "to stand".

丶　二　立　立　立　站　站　站　站　站

站

空 　　kōng　empty, hollow

空气　kōngqì　air
天空　tiānkōng　sky
空中　kōngzhōng　in the sky

穴 ＋ 工 → 空

　　"穴"是形旁，表示和洞穴有关，"工"［gōng］作声旁。"洞穴"里面是"空"的。
The signific "穴" (hole) indicates that the word has something to do with a hole. "工" is the phonetic. A hole is hollow and empty inside.

| 丶 | 八 | 宀 | 宀 | 穴 | 空 | 空 | 空 | | | |
|---|---|---|---|---|---|---|---|---|---|---|
| 空 | | | | | | | | | | |

聋 　　lóng　deaf

聋子　lóngzi　a deaf person
聋哑　lóngyǎ　deaf and dumb
耳聋　ěrlóng　deaf

龙 ＋ 耳 → 聋

　　"龙"［lóng］是声旁，"耳"作形旁。"耳朵"听不见声音叫"聋"。
"龙" is the phonetic. "耳" (ear) is the signific. When the ears do not hear one is deaf.

| 一 | ナ | 九 | 龙 | 龙 | 龙 | 耸 | 聋 | 聋 | 聋 | 聋 |
|---|---|---|---|---|---|---|---|---|---|---|
| 聋 | | | | | | | | | | |

129

# 顶

**dǐng   top, peak, crown**

| | | |
|---|---|---|
| 房顶 | fángdǐng | roof |
| 屋顶 | wūdǐng | roof |
| 顶头 | dǐngtóu | top, end |

丁 + 页 → 顶

　　"丁"[ dǐng ] 是声旁，"页"作形旁，表示和"头"有关。物体最上面的部分叫"顶"。

"丁" is the phonetic. The significic "页" indicates that the word has to do with the head of something. The highest end of something is its top or peak.

| 一 | 丁 | 厂 | 丁 | 丌 | 顶 | 顶 | 顶 | | | |
|---|---|---|---|---|---|---|---|---|---|---|

| 顶 | | | | | | | | | | |
|---|---|---|---|---|---|---|---|---|---|---|


# 蚊

**wén   mosquito**

| | | |
|---|---|---|
| 蚊子 | wénzi | mosquito |
| 蚊帐 | wénzhàng | mosquito net |
| 蚊蝇 | wényíng | mosquitos and flies |

虫 + 文 → 蚊

　　"虫"是形旁，"文"[ wén ] 作声旁。"蚊子"是一种"昆虫"。

"虫" (insect) is signific. "文" is the phonetic. A mosquito is a type of insect.

| 丶 | 丶口 | 口 | 中 | 虫 | 虫 | 虫 | 虾 | 虾 | 蚊 | |
|---|---|---|---|---|---|---|---|---|---|---|

| 蚊 | | | | | | | | | | |
|---|---|---|---|---|---|---|---|---|---|---|

筷　　kuài　chopsticks

| 筷子 | kuàizi | chopsticks |
|------|--------|------------|
| 碗筷 | wǎnkuài | bowls and chopsticks |
| 火筷 | huǒkuài | fire-tongs |

⺮ ＋ 快 → 筷

"⺮"是"竹"的变体,作形旁,"快"[ kuài ]是声旁。"筷子"是用"竹子"作的。

The signific "⺮" is a variant of "竹" (bamboo) and "快" is the phonetic. Chopsticks are made of bamboo.

| ノ | ト | ⺦ | ⺮ | 竺 | 竿 | 笁 | 笁 | 筶 | 筷 | 筷 |
|---|---|---|---|---|---|---|---|---|---|---|

| 筷 | | | | | | | | | | |

---

舰 [艦]　　jiàn　warship

| 舰艇 | jiàntǐng | naval vessels |
|------|----------|---------------|
| 军舰 | jūnjiàn | warship |
| 舰船 | jiànchuán | warships |

舟 ＋ 见 → 舰

"舟"是形旁,表示和船有关,"见"[ jiàn ]是声旁。"军舰"是"船"的一种。

The signific "舟" (boat) shows that the word has to do with ships. "见" is the phonetic. A warship is of course a type of ship.

| ノ | 丿 | 刀 | 冎 | 舟 | 舟 | 舥 | 舮 | 舮 | 舰 |
|---|---|---|---|---|---|---|---|---|---|

| 舰 | | | | | | | | | |

裤 [褲]　　kù　trousers

裤子　　kùzi　　trousers
短裤　　duǎnkù　short
裤衩　　kùchǎ　underpants

裤　+　库　→　裤

　"衤"是"衣"字的变体,作形旁,表示和衣服有关,"库"[ kù ]是声旁。"裤子"是服装的一种。
"衤" is a variant of "衣"(clothing). As signific it indicates the relationship to clothing. "库"is the phonetic. A pair of trousers is a piece of clothing.

| 丶 | 冫 | 衤 | 衤 | 衤 | 矿 | 矿 | 裤 | 裤 | 裤 | |
|---|---|---|---|---|---|---|---|---|---|---|

| 裤 | | | | | | | | | | |

粮　　liáng　grain, cereal

粮食　　liángshi　　grain
粮店　　liángdiàn　grain shop
细粮　　xìliáng　　flour and rice

米　+　良　→　粮

　"米"是形旁,表示和粮食有关,"良"[ liáng ]作声旁。
The signific "米" indicates that the word refers to cereals. "良"is the phonetic.

| 米 | 米 | 籿 | 籿 | 籵 | 粮 | 粮 | 粮 | | |
|---|---|---|---|---|---|---|---|---|---|

| 粮 | | | | | | | | | |

132

# 超

chāo    surpass, overtake

| 超过 | chāoguò | surpass |
| 超越 | chāoyuè | surmount |
| 超额 | chāo'é | above quota |

走 ＋ 召 → 超

"走"是形旁，表示和行走有关，"召"[ zhāo ]作声旁。"走"得快才可以"超"过别人。

The signific "走" shows that the word has to do with walking. "召" is the phonetic. When one walks fast one may surpass other people.

| 一 | 十 | 土 | 十 | 赤 | 走 | 走 | 起 | 起 | 超 |

| 超 | | | | | | | | | |

# 跑

pǎo    run

| 跑步 | pǎobù | run |
| 长跑 | chángpǎo | long-distance race |
| 短跑 | duǎnpǎo | dash |

足 ＋ 包 → 跑

"⻊"是"足"的变体，作形旁，表示和脚的动作有关，"包"[ bāo ]是声旁。"跑步"要用"脚"。

The signific "⻊" is a variant of "足"and indicates that the word has to do with activities of the feet. "包" is the phonetic. One uses his feet to run.

| 𧾷 | 𧾷 | 趵 | 趵 | 趵 | 跑 | | | | |

| 跑 | | | | | | | | | |

133

讲 [講]　　　jiǎng　speak

讲话　jiǎnghuà　speak
讲课　jiǎngkè　teach
讲解　jiǎngjié　explain

讠 + 井 → 讲

"讠"是"言"字的变体,作形旁,表示和讲话有关,"井"[ jīng ]是声旁。

The signific "讠"is a variant of "言"(language) and indicates that the word has to do with talking. "井" is the phonetic.

| 丶 | 讠 | 讠 | 讠 | 讲 | 讲 | | | | |
|---|---|---|---|---|---|---|---|---|---|

| 讲 | | | | | | | | | |
|---|---|---|---|---|---|---|---|---|---|

雾　　　wù　fog

下雾　xiàwù　It's getting foggy
云雾　yúnwù　clouds and mist
雾气　wùqì　fog

雨 + 务 → 雾

"雨"是形旁,表示和云雨现象有关,"务"[ wù ]是声旁。

The signific "雨" (rain) shows that the word has something to do with rain, meteorological phenomena. "务"is the phonetic.

| 一 | 亠 | 示 | 示 | 雨 | 雫 | 雫 | 雯 | 雾 | 雾 |
|---|---|---|---|---|---|---|---|---|---|

| 雾 | | | | | | | | | |
|---|---|---|---|---|---|---|---|---|---|

134

钢 [鋼]　　　**gāng　steel**　　钢铁　gāngtiě　iron and steel
　　　　　　　　　　　　　　　钢笔　gāngbǐ　pen
　　　　　　　　　　　　　　　钢琴　gāngqín　piano

钅 ＋ 冈 → 钢

　　"钅"是"金"字的变体,作形旁,表示和金属有关,"冈"[gāng]是声旁。
The signific "钅", a variant of "金"(gold), indicates that the word has to do with metals. "冈" is the phonetic.

| 丿 | 𠂊 | 钅 | 钅 | 钅 | 钅 | 钅 | 钢 | | | |
|---|---|---|---|---|---|---|---|---|---|---|

| 钢 | | | | | | | | | | |
|---|---|---|---|---|---|---|---|---|---|---|

饭 [飯]　　　**fàn　meal**　　吃饭　chīfàn　eat
　　　　　　　　　　　　　　　饭店　fàndiàn　hotel
　　　　　　　　　　　　　　　饭馆　fànguǎn　restaurant

饣 ＋ 反 → 饭

　　"饣"是"食"字的变体,作形旁,表示和饮食有关,"反"[fàn]是声旁。"饭"是"食物"。
The signific "饣" is a variant of "食"(food) and indicates that the word has to do with food. "反" is the phonetic. Meal is a type of food.

| 丿 | 𠂊 | 饣 | 饣 | 饣 | 饭 | 饭 | | | | |
|---|---|---|---|---|---|---|---|---|---|---|

| 饭 | | | | | | | | | | |
|---|---|---|---|---|---|---|---|---|---|---|

醒　xǐng　sober up, wake up

睡醒　shuìxǐng　wake up
觉醒　juéxǐng　awaken
醒悟　xǐngwù　wake up

酉 + 星 → 醒

"酉"古代的写法像酒器,作形旁,表示和酒有关,"星"[xīng]是声旁。人刚醒时象喝过酒一样。
The ancient form of "酉" shows a drinking vessel. As signific it indicates that the word has to do with wine. "星" is the phonetic. When one wakes up he feels as if he just had a drink.

| 一 | 厂 | 冂 | 厉 | 西 | 酉 | 酉 | 酲 | 酲 | 醒 |
|---|---|---|---|---|---|---|---|---|---|

| 醒 | | | | | | | | | |
|---|---|---|---|---|---|---|---|---|---|

飘 [飄] piāo　wave, float, flutter

飘扬　piāoyáng　wave
飘荡　piāodàng　drift
飘带　piāodài　streamer

票 + 风 → 飘

"票"[piào]是声旁,"风"是形旁,表示和空气的流动有关。有"风",东西才能飘起来。
"票" is the phonetic. The signific "风"(wind) indicates that the word has to do with wind. Only when there is wind can things flutter.

| 一 | 覀 | 覀 | 西 | 西 | 票 | 票 | 飘 | 飘 | 飘 |
|---|---|---|---|---|---|---|---|---|---|

| 飘 | | | | | | | | | |
|---|---|---|---|---|---|---|---|---|---|

136

# 瓷

cí   porcelain

瓷器　cíqì　porcelain
陶瓷　táocí　ceramics
瓷碗　cíwǎn　china bowl

$$次 + 瓦 → 瓷$$

　　"次"[ cì ]是声旁，"瓦"作形旁，表示和陶土制品有关。"瓷器"是由"陶土"烧制而成。
"次"is the phonetic. The significant "瓦"( tile ) indicates something made from clay. Porcelain is produced from a certain kind of clay.

| 丶 | ⼎ | ⼎ | 次 | 次 | 次 | 瓷 | 瓷 | 瓷 | 瓷 | |

| 瓷 | | | | | | | | | | |

# 鞭

biān   whip, lash

鞭子　biānzi　whip
皮鞭　píbiān　leather-thonged whip
马鞭　mǎbiān　horsewhip

$$革 + 便 → 鞭$$

　　"革"是形旁，表示和皮革有关，"便"[ biàn ]作声旁。"鞭子"是用"皮子"作的。
The significant "革"( leather ) indicates that the word has to do with leather. "便"is the phonetic. A whip is made of leather.

| 一 | 廿 | 廿 | 苫 | 革 | 靯 | 靪 | 鞭 | 鞭 | 鞭 | |

| 鞭 | | | | | | | | | | |

# 7

## 部首和汉字

### RADICALS AND CHINESE CHARACTERS

#### 部首

汉语字典、词典根据汉字形体偏旁分成不同的门类,如"口部""山部""木部""火部"等,这些门类叫部首。

某一部首里的字,有独体字,也有合体字;有象形字和指事字,也有会意字和形声字。它们所具有的同一偏旁,有的作形旁表意,有的作声旁表音,有的是只是字一个笔画或一个替代符号。了解和掌握汉字的部首以及某一部首中偏旁的作用,对于记忆汉字和查阅字典、词典都是十分有用的。

对于一个不认识的字,首先分析它的偏旁,看它是属于什么部首的字,然后在部首检字表内,通过字的笔画数找到这个字的页码。如:"吃"字。【口部】三画,见 164 页(《现代汉语词典》修订本)。

汉字的部首有三类:1. 成字部首,如"木""口""大"等;2. 偏旁部首,如"阝""宀""辶"等,只作偏旁,不作为汉字使用,它们多是某些独体字的变体;3. 笔画部首,如"丿""丨""、"等。

汉字的部首有 200 个左右,本讲只介绍七十三个常用部首。

#### Radicals（Bushou）

In Chinese dictionaries, Chinese characters are arranged according to the different components that are composed of. Components that are used in this way are called "radicals" (*Bushou*), e.g. "mouth radical"（口部）"mountain radical"（山部）"tree radical"（木部）"fire radical"（火部）and so forth.

Under one radical there may be grouped independent characters and combined characters; or pictograms, indicative characters , associative characters and pictophonograms. The component that have in common may serve as signific in some and as phonetic in others characters. It may even be just a stroke or a symbol, as is often the case with simplified characters. To understand and be able to use the radicals and their respective functions in different characters is useful both for the memorization of characters and for the use of dictionaries. When one encounters an unknown character, one first analyzes it to find which component is its radical and count the remaining strokes. Then you look for the radical in the dictionary's radical index and under it for the characters with the required stroke number. Among them you will find the character you want and its page number. e.g.

"吃": mouth radical "口", 3 strokes, p.164. (in Modern Chinese Dictionary 1996)

There are three styls of radicals: 1, Radicals which are characters by themselves, e.g. "木""口""大" etc. 2, Radicals which are character components only, not used as independent characters, e.g. "阝""宀""亻" etc. Most of them are variants of independent characters. 3, Radicals that consist of one stroke only, e.g. "丿""丨""、".

In the dictionary there are usually about 200 radicals. This chapter introduces 73 common ones.

# 【人部】

"人"象形字,二画,见 6 页 。"人"作形旁的字多和人有关。人字旁在左侧时写作"亻"。

"人" is a 2 stroke pictogram (see p.6). The pictophonograms composed of the signific "人" refer to the human being. When placed on the left side, the signific "人" is written as "亻".

个　gè　(measure word)

| 一个 | yī gè | one |
| 个人 | gèrén | individual |
| 个子 | gèzi | height |

| 个 | | | | | | | | | |
|---|---|---|---|---|---|---|---|---|---|

全　quán　complete, whole

| 全体 | quǎntǐ | all, entire |
| 全国 | quánguó | the whole nation |
| 全家 | quánjiā | the whole family |

| 全 | | | | | | | | | |
|---|---|---|---|---|---|---|---|---|---|

会　huì　meeting, can

| 会见 | huìjiàn | meet with |
| 开会 | kāihuì | hold a meeting |
| 会说 | huì shuō | can speak |

| 会 | | | | | | | | | |
|---|---|---|---|---|---|---|---|---|---|

他　tā　he

| 他们 | tamen | they |
| 他的 | tade | his |
| 其他 | qita | other |

| 他 | | | | | | | | | |
|---|---|---|---|---|---|---|---|---|---|

你　nǐ　you

| 你们 | nǐmen | you(plural) |
| 你的 | nǐde | your |
| 你好 | nǐhǎo | hello |

| 你 | | | | | | | | | |
|---|---|---|---|---|---|---|---|---|---|

们　men　(suffix)

| 我们 | wǒmen | we |
| 她们 | tāmen | they |
| 人们 | rénmen | people |

| 们 | | | | | | | | | |
|---|---|---|---|---|---|---|---|---|---|

作　　zuò　　to do

工作 gōngzuò　work
作家 zuòjiā　writer
作者 zuòzhě　author

| 作 | | | | | | | | | |
|---|---|---|---|---|---|---|---|---|---|

## 【刀部】

"刀"象形字，二画，见 8 页。"刀"作形旁的字大多与剪裁、切割的意思有关。刀字旁在右侧时写作"刂"。

"刀" is a 2 stroke pictogram (see page 8). In most cases, the pictophonograms composed of the signific "刀" refer to cutting, carving, etc. When placed on the right side, "刀" is written as "刂".

切　　qiē　　cut, slice

切开 qiēkāi　incision
切除 qiēchú　excision
切断 qiēduàn　cut off

| 切 | | | | | | | | | |
|---|---|---|---|---|---|---|---|---|---|

刚　　gāng　　firm, just

刚强 gāngqiáng　firm
刚才 gāngcái　just now
刚好 gānghǎo　exactly

| 刚 | | | | | | | | | |
|---|---|---|---|---|---|---|---|---|---|

别　　bié　　leave, other

分别 fēnbié　part
区别 qūbié　distinguish
别的 biéde　other

| 别 | | | | | | | | | |
|---|---|---|---|---|---|---|---|---|---|

刻　　kè　　carve, a quarter

石刻 shíkè　carved stone
时刻 shíkè　moment
立刻 lìkè　at once

| 刻 | | | | | | | | | |
|---|---|---|---|---|---|---|---|---|---|

到　　dào　　arrive, go to

到达 dàodá　arrive
到处 dàochù　at all places
到期 dàoqī　become due

| 到 | | | | | | | | | |
|---|---|---|---|---|---|---|---|---|---|

# 【力部】

"力"象形字，二画，见 8 页。"力"作形旁的字大多与力气、力量的意思有关。力字旁的位置比较灵活。

"力" is a 2 stroke pictogram（see page 8）. In most cases, the pictophonograms composed of the signific "力" refer to strength or power. Its position is flexible.

动　dòng　move

| 运动 | yùndòng | sports |
| 动物 | dòngwù | animal |
| 活动 | huódòng | activity |

| 动 | | | | | | | | | |
|---|---|---|---|---|---|---|---|---|---|
| | | | | | | | | | |

助　zhù　help, assist

| 帮助 | bāngzhù | help |
| 协助 | xiézhù | assist |
| 助手 | zhùshǒu | assistant |

| 助 | | | | | | | | | |
|---|---|---|---|---|---|---|---|---|---|
| | | | | | | | | | |

加　jiā　add, plus

| 加强 | jiāqiáng | strengthen |
| 加法 | jiāfǎ | addition |
| 增加 | zēngjiā | increase |

| 加 | | | | | | | | | |
|---|---|---|---|---|---|---|---|---|---|
| | | | | | | | | | |

办　bàn　handle

| 办法 | bànfǎ | way |
| 办事 | bànshì | handle affairs |
| 办理 | bànlǐ | handle |

| 办 | | | | | | | | | |
|---|---|---|---|---|---|---|---|---|---|
| | | | | | | | | | |

# 【冫部】

"冫"偏旁部首，二画，一般在左侧。"冫"作形旁的字多和寒冷的意思有关。

"冫" is a 2 stroke component. It's usually placed on the left side. The pictophonograms composed of this signific have something to do with cold.

冷　lěng　cold

| 寒冷 | hánlěng | cold, frigid |
| 冰冷 | bīnglěng | ice-cold |
| 冷静 | lěngjìng | sober |

| 冷 | | | | | | | | | |
|---|---|---|---|---|---|---|---|---|---|
| | | | | | | | | | |

**凉**    liáng      cool

| 凉快 | liángkuai | nice and cool |
| 冰凉 | bīngliáng | ice-cold |
| 凉水 | liángshuǐ | cold water |

| 凉 | | | | | | | | | |
|---|---|---|---|---|---|---|---|---|---|

**次**    cì      order, inferior, time

| 每次 | měi cì | every time |
| 名次 | míngcì | position in a name list |
| 次品 | cìpǐn | substandard products |

| 次 | | | | | | | | | |
|---|---|---|---|---|---|---|---|---|---|

**净**    jìng      clean

| 干净 | gānjìng | clean |
| 清净 | qīngjìng | peace and quiet |
| 纯净 | chúnjìng | pure |

| 净 | | | | | | | | | |
|---|---|---|---|---|---|---|---|---|---|

**准**    zhǔn      allow, norm, exact

| 准备 | zhǔnbèi | prepare |
| 准时 | zhǔnshí | on time |
| 批准 | pīzhǔn | approve |

| 准 | | | | | | | | | |
|---|---|---|---|---|---|---|---|---|---|

## 【又部】

"又"象形字,二画,见 22 页。"又"作形旁的字有的和手的动作有关。在简化字中只作为一个符号。又字旁的位置比较灵活。

"又" is a 2 stroke pictogram (see p. 22). Some pictophonograms composed of this signific refer to movement, gesture of the hand. It is used as a symbol in the simplified Chinese characters. Its position is flexible.

**对**    duì      treat, right

| 对面 | duìmiàn | opposite |
| 对比 | duìbǐ | contrast |
| 对立 | duìlì | oppose |

| 对 | | | | | | | | | |
|---|---|---|---|---|---|---|---|---|---|

**欢**    huān      joyous

| 喜欢 | xǐhuān | like |
| 欢乐 | huānlè | happy |
| 欢喜 | huānxǐ | joyful |

| 欢 | | | | | | | | | |
|---|---|---|---|---|---|---|---|---|---|

难　　nán　　difficult

困难 kùnnán difficult
艰难 jiānnán hard, difficult
难看 nánkàn ugly

| 难 | | | | | | | | | |
|---|---|---|---|---|---|---|---|---|---|

变　　biàn　　change

变化 biànhuà change
转变 zhuǎnbiàn transform
演变 yǎnbiàn evolve

| 变 | | | | | | | | | |
|---|---|---|---|---|---|---|---|---|---|

发　　fā　　send out, develop

出发 chūfā set out
发展 fāzhǎn develop
发表 fābiǎo publish

| 发 | | | | | | | | | |
|---|---|---|---|---|---|---|---|---|---|

## 【阝部】

"阝"偏旁部首,二画,有两个位置,一个在右侧,一个在左侧。
"阝"在右侧的字多与城邑、地区有关。"阝"在左侧的字多和山坡、地势的意思有关。

"阝" is a 2 stroke component. As signific it has two positions. The pictophograms composed of it on the right side refer to the city-state, and those on the left side refer to the hill or terrain.

那　　nà　　that

那样 nàyàng of that kind
那些 nàxiē those
那么 nàme like that

| 那 | | | | | | | | | |
|---|---|---|---|---|---|---|---|---|---|

都　　dū　　capital

首都 shǒudū capital
都市 dūshì city
都城 dūchéng capital

| 都 | | | | | | | | | |
|---|---|---|---|---|---|---|---|---|---|

部　　bù　　part, unit

部队 bùduì army
部分 bùfen part
全部 quánbù whole, all

| 部 | | | | | | | | | |
|---|---|---|---|---|---|---|---|---|---|

143

院　　yuàn　　courtyard

院子 yuànzi　　courtyard
学院 xuéyuàn　　college
院长 yuànzhǎng　college director

| 院 | | | | | | | | | |
|---|---|---|---|---|---|---|---|---|---|

际　　jì　　border, between

国际 guójì　　international
交际 jiāojì　　communication
边际 biānjì　　limit

| 际 | | | | | | | | | |
|---|---|---|---|---|---|---|---|---|---|

除　　chú　　get rid of, except

切除 qiēchú　　excision
消除 xiāochú　　eliminate
消除 qīngchú　　clear away

| 除 | | | | | | | | | |
|---|---|---|---|---|---|---|---|---|---|

队　　duì　　team, group

队伍 duìwu　　troops
球队 qiúduì　　team
队员 duìyuán　team member

| 队 | | | | | | | | | |
|---|---|---|---|---|---|---|---|---|---|

# 【土部】

"土"象形字,三画,见 16 页。"土"作形旁的字多和土有关。土字旁在左侧时写作"⻂"。

"土" is a 3 stroke pictogram (see page 16). In most cases, the pictophonograms composed of the signific "土" refer to soil. When placed on the left side, "土" is written as "⻂".

在　　zài　　exist

现在 xiànzài　　now
正在 zhèngzài　in process of
存在 cúnzài　　exist

| 在 | | | | | | | | | |
|---|---|---|---|---|---|---|---|---|---|

堂　　táng　　a hall

食堂 shítáng　　dining hall
礼堂 lǐtáng　　assembly hall
教堂 jiàotáng　church

| 堂 | | | | | | | | | |
|---|---|---|---|---|---|---|---|---|---|

地   dì   land, soil

地方 dìfang   locality
地球 dìqiú   the earth
土地 tǔdì   land

| 地 | | | | | | | | | |
|---|---|---|---|---|---|---|---|---|---|

场   cǎng   place, farm

操场 cāochǎng   playground
剧场 jùchǎng   theatre
球场 qiúchǎng   court, fields

| 场 | | | | | | | | | |
|---|---|---|---|---|---|---|---|---|---|

块   kuài   piece

方块 fāngkuài   square
土块 tǔkuài   clod
石块 shíkuài   stone

| 块 | | | | | | | | | |
|---|---|---|---|---|---|---|---|---|---|

墙   qiáng   wall

城墙 chéngqiáng   city wall
墙上 qiángshàng   on the wall
墙壁 qiángbì   wall

| 墙 | | | | | | | | | |
|---|---|---|---|---|---|---|---|---|---|

## 【工部】

"工"象形字，三画，见 16 页。"工"字在形声字中主要作声旁。工字旁位置比较灵活。工字旁在左侧时写作"工"。

"工" is a 3 stroke pictogram (see page 16). In most cases, it's used as the phonetic of pictophonograms. Its position is flexible. When placed on the left side, "工" is written as "工".

贡   gòng   **tribute**

贡献 gòngxiàn   contribute
进贡 jìngòng   pay tribute
贡品 gòngpǐn   articles of tribute

| 贡 | | | | | | | | | |
|---|---|---|---|---|---|---|---|---|---|

功   gōng   **merit, result, work**

功能 gōngnéng   function
功课 gōngkè   schoolwork
用功 yònggōng   hardworking

| | | | | | | | | | |
|---|---|---|---|---|---|---|---|---|---|

# 【大部】

"大"象形字，三画，见 6 页。大字旁在形声字中的位置可上，可下。
"大" is a 3 stroke pictogram (see page 6). As a component of the pictophonograms, it may be placed on the top or at the bottom.

奇　qí　strange, surprise

奇怪 qíguài　strange
奇妙 qímiào　marvellous
新奇 xīnqí　strange, new

| 奇 | | | | | | | | | |
|---|---|---|---|---|---|---|---|---|---|

奋　fèn　exert oneself

奋斗 fèndòu　struggle
勤奋 qínfèn　diligent
兴奋 xīngfèn　be excited

| 奋 | | | | | | | | | |
|---|---|---|---|---|---|---|---|---|---|

套　tào　sheath, cover with

套子 tàozi　sheath
客套 kètào　polite remarks
一套 yītào　a set of

| 套 | | | | | | | | | |
|---|---|---|---|---|---|---|---|---|---|

# 【口部】

"口"象形字，三画，见 10 页。"口"作形旁的字一般和口的动作有关。
口字旁在字的左侧时写得小一点。
"口" is a 3 stroke pictogram (see page 10). In most cases, the pictophonograms composed of the signific: "口" refer to the movement of mouth. When placed on the left side, "口" is written smaller.

吃　chī　eat

吃饭 chī fàn　eat, have a meal
好吃 hǎochī　good to eat
吃力 chīlì　be a strain

| 吃 | | | | | | | | | |
|---|---|---|---|---|---|---|---|---|---|

喝　hē　drink

喝酒 hē jiǔ　drink wine
喝茶 hē chá　drink tea
好喝 hǎohē　good to drink

| 喝 | | | | | | | | | |
|---|---|---|---|---|---|---|---|---|---|

叫　jiào　cry, call

喊叫 hǎnjiào　shout
叫唤 jiàohuan　cry out
叫座 jiàozuò　draw well

| 叫 | | | | | | | | | |
|---|---|---|---|---|---|---|---|---|---|

听　tīng　listen, hear

听说 tīngshuō　be told
听话 tīnghuà　be obedient
好听 hǎotīng　pleasant to hear

| 听 | | | | | | | | | |
|---|---|---|---|---|---|---|---|---|---|

哑　yǎ　mute

哑巴 yǎba　mute
聋哑 lóngyǎ　deaf-mute
哑语 yǎyǔ　sign language

| 哑 | | | | | | | | | |
|---|---|---|---|---|---|---|---|---|---|

告　gào　tell

告诉 gàosu　tell
转告 zhuǎngào　transmit
布告 bùgào　notice

| 告 | | | | | | | | | |
|---|---|---|---|---|---|---|---|---|---|

# 【口部】

"口"偏旁部首,三画,像个方形的框框,"口"作形旁表示一定的界限和范围。
"口" is a 3 stroke component. It resembles a square box. As signific "口" signifies limits and scope.

圆　yuán　round, circle

圆形 yuánxíng　circular
圆心 yuánxīn　the centre of a circle
圆满 yuánmǎn　satisfactory

| 圆 | | | | | | | | | |
|---|---|---|---|---|---|---|---|---|---|

图　tú　picture, map

地图 dìtú　map
图片 túpiàn　picture
图形 túxíng　graph

| 图 | | | | | | | | | |
|---|---|---|---|---|---|---|---|---|---|

围　wéi　enclose, all round

周围 zhōuwéi　all round
包围 bāowéi　surround
围巾 wéijīn　muffler

| 围 | | | | | | | | | | |
|---|---|---|---|---|---|---|---|---|---|---|

## 【巾部】

"巾"象形字,三画,见 17 页。"巾"作形旁的字大多和巾一样的织物有关。巾字旁的位置比较灵活,在左侧时写成瘦长形。

"巾" is a 3 stroke pictogram (see page 17). In most cases, the pictophonograms composed of the signific "巾" refer to fabrics which are like muffler. When placed on the left side, "巾" is written thinner. Its position is flexible.

布　bù　cloth

棉布 miánbù　cotton
布鞋 bùxié　cloth shoes
分布 fēnbù　be distributed

| 布 | | | | | | | | | | |
|---|---|---|---|---|---|---|---|---|---|---|

带　dài　belt, band, take

带子 dàizi　belt
领带 lǐngdài　necktie
皮带 pídài　leather belt

| 带 | | | | | | | | | | |
|---|---|---|---|---|---|---|---|---|---|---|

帮　bāng　help

鞋帮 xiébāng　upper of a shoe
帮助 bāngzhù　help
帮忙 bāngmáng　give a hand

| 帮 | | | | | | | | | | |
|---|---|---|---|---|---|---|---|---|---|---|

## 【山部】

"山"象形字,三画,见 17 页。"山"作形旁的字大多和山有关。山字旁的位置比较灵活。

"山" is a 3 stroke pictogram (see page 17). In most cases, the pictophonograms composed of the signific "山" have to do with the mountain. Its position is flexible.

岸　àn　bank, shore

海岸 hǎi'àn　coast
河岸 héàn　the bank of a river
上岸 shàng àn　go ashore

| 岸 | | | | | | | | | | |
|---|---|---|---|---|---|---|---|---|---|---|

岛 | dǎo | island | 海岛 hǎidǎo | island
半岛 bàndǎo | peninsula
群岛 qúndǎo | archipelago

| 岛 | | | | | | | | | |

峰 | fēng | peak, summit | 山峰 shānfēng | mountain peak
险峰 xiǎnfēng | perilous peak
高峰 gāofēng | peak

| 峰 | | | | | | | | | |

## 【彳部】

"彳"是"行"字的左半边,"行"是个象形字,见 36 页。"彳"作形旁的字大多和道路、行走、行动有关。偏旁"彳"总在字的左侧。
"彳" is half of "行". "行" is a pictogram (see p. 36). In most cases, the pictophonograms composed of the signific "彳" refer to road, walking and movement. It's always on the left side.

往 | wǎng | go, toward | 来往 láiwǎng | come and go
往年 wǎngnián | former years
往返 wǎngfǎn | go there and back

| 往 | | | | | | | | | |

街 | jiē | street | 街道 jiēdào | street
大街 dàjiē | main street
街上 jiēshang | on the street

| 街 | | | | | | | | | |

很 | hěn | very | 很好 hěn hǎo | very good
很多 hěn duō | many
很大 hěn dà | very big

| 很 | | | | | | | | | |

得 | dé | get, obtain | 得到 dédào | get
获得 huòdé | obtain
取得 qǔdé | gain

| 得 | | | | | | | | | |

# 【彡部】

"彡"象形符号,三画。"彡"作形旁的字和毛须、光芒等有关。偏旁"彡"一般在字的左侧,有时在右侧。

"彡" is a 3 stroke component. The pictophongrams composed of the signific "彡" refer to the hair and rays of light. "彡" is usually on the left side.

形　xíng　form, shape

形状 xíngzhuàng　form
形象 síngxiàng　image
体形 tǐxíng　bodily form

| 形 | | | | | | | | | | |
|---|---|---|---|---|---|---|---|---|---|---|

影　yǐng　shadow

影子 yǐngzi　shadow
电影 diànyǐng　film
影响 yǐngxiǎng　influence

| 影 | | | | | | | | | | |
|---|---|---|---|---|---|---|---|---|---|---|

须　xū　beard, must

须子 xūzi　palpus
胡须 húxū　beard
必须 bìxū　must

| 须 | | | | | | | | | | |
|---|---|---|---|---|---|---|---|---|---|---|

# 【夂部】

"夂"偏旁部首,三画。"夂"作形旁的字多与行动、运行有关。偏旁"夂"的位置比较灵活。

"夂" is a 3 stroke component. The pictophonograms composed of the signific "夂" generally refer to movement and motion. Its position is flexible.

处　chǔ　get along, handle

处理 chǔlǐ　handle
处事 chǔshì　handle affairs
处分 chǔfèn　punish

| 处 | | | | | | | | | | |
|---|---|---|---|---|---|---|---|---|---|---|

备　bèi　prepare, provide

准备 zhǔnbèi　prepare
备用 bèiyòng　spare
预备 yùbèi　get ready

| 备 | | | | | | | | | | |
|---|---|---|---|---|---|---|---|---|---|---|

| 务 | wù | be engaged in | 服务 fúwù | serve |
| | | | 家务 jiāwù | household duties |
| | | | 事务 shìwù | work |

| 务 | | | | | | | | | |
|---|---|---|---|---|---|---|---|---|---|

| 夏 | xià | summer | 夏天 xiàtiān | summer |
| | | | 夏日 xiàrì | summer |
| | | | 夏季 xiàjì | summer |

| 夏 | | | | | | | | | |
|---|---|---|---|---|---|---|---|---|---|

## 【广部】

"广"象形字,三画,见11页。"广"作形旁的字多和房屋、殿堂有关。偏旁广的位置很固定。

"广" is a 3 stroke pictogram (see p. 11). The pictophonograms composed of the signific "广" usually refer to the house and hall. Its position is fixed.

| 店 | diàn | shop, store, inn | 商店 shāngdiàn | shop |
| | | | 饭店 fàndiàn | hotel |
| | | | 书店 shūdiàn | bookshop |

| 店 | | | | | | | | | |
|---|---|---|---|---|---|---|---|---|---|

| 府 | fǔ | seat of government | 政府 zhèngfǔ | government |
| | | | 官府 guānfǔ | local authorities |
| | | | 首府 shǒufǔ | capital |

| 府 | | | | | | | | | |
|---|---|---|---|---|---|---|---|---|---|

| 度 | dù | degree | 温度 wēndù | temperature |
| | | | 高度 gāodù | height |
| | | | 长度 chángdù | length |

| 度 | | | | | | | | | |
|---|---|---|---|---|---|---|---|---|---|

| 应 | yīng | should, answer | 应该 yīnggāi | should |
| | | | 应当 yīngdāng | should |
| | | | 应有 yīngyǒu | due |

| 应 | | | | | | | | | |
|---|---|---|---|---|---|---|---|---|---|

# 【门部】

"门"象形字，三画，见 15 页。"门"作形旁的字多和门有关。门字旁的位置很固定。

"门" is a 3 stroke pictogram (see p. 15). The pictophonograms composed of the signific "门" usually have something to do with the door. Its position is fixed.

**闭** bì close, shut

| 关闭 guānbì | close |
| 封闭 fēngbì | seal off |
| 闭幕 bìmù | the curtain falls |

| 闭 | | | | | | | | |
|---|---|---|---|---|---|---|---|---|

**间** jiān room, space

| 房间 fángjiān | room |
| 时间 shíjiān | time |
| 空间 kōngjiān | space |

| 间 | | | | | | | | |
|---|---|---|---|---|---|---|---|---|

**闹** nào noisy

| 热闹 rènào | lively |
| 闹市 nàoshì | busy streets |
| 闹钟 nàozhōng | alarm clock |

| 闹 | | | | | | | | |
|---|---|---|---|---|---|---|---|---|

# 【宀部】

"宀"偏旁部首，三画。"宀"作形旁的字大多和房间有关。偏旁"宀"总在字的上部。

"宀" is a 3 stroke component. The pictophonograms composed of the signific "宀" usually have to do with the room. It's always placed on the top.

**宿** sù lodge for the night

| 宿舍 sùshè | dormitory |
| 住宿 zhùsù | stay |
| 宿愿 sùyuàn | long-cherished wish |

| 宿 | | | | | | | | |
|---|---|---|---|---|---|---|---|---|

**完** wán finish, run out

| 完全 wánquán | complete |
| 完整 wánzhěng | complete |
| 完成 wánchéng | accomplish |

| 完 | | | | | | | | |
|---|---|---|---|---|---|---|---|---|

字    zì      character

汉字 hànzì   Chinese character
名字 míngzi   name
字典 zìdiǎn   dictionary

| 字 | | | | | | | | | |
|---|---|---|---|---|---|---|---|---|---|

定    dìng      calm, fix

决定 juédìng   decide
一定 yídìng   certainly
肯定 kěndìng   affirm

| 定 | | | | | | | | | |
|---|---|---|---|---|---|---|---|---|---|

## 【尸部】

"尸"象形字,三画,见 22 页。"尸"作形旁的字和人体或人体的活动有关。尸字旁的位置比较固定。

"尸" is a 3 stroke pictogram (see p. 22). The pictophonograms composed of the signific "尸" usually refer to the body or the movement of the body. Its position is fixed.

居    jū      reside

居住 jūzhù   live
居民 jūmín   resident
居留 jūliú   reside

| 居 | | | | | | | | | |
|---|---|---|---|---|---|---|---|---|---|

展    zhǎn      open up

发展 fāzhǎn   develop
展览 zhǎnlǎn   exhibit
开展 kāizhǎn   launch

| 展 | | | | | | | | | |
|---|---|---|---|---|---|---|---|---|---|

局    jú      office, part

邮局 yóujú   post office
局部 júbù   part
局面 júmiàn   aspect

| 局 | | | | | | | | | |
|---|---|---|---|---|---|---|---|---|---|

层    céng      layer, storey

一层 yī céng   the ground floor
层层 céngcéng   layer upon layer
层次 céngcì   arrangement of ideas

| 层 | | | | | | | | | |
|---|---|---|---|---|---|---|---|---|---|

# 【弓部】

"弓"象形字,三画,见 28 页。"弓"作形旁的字多和弓箭有关。弓字旁一般在字的左侧。

"弓" is a 3 stroke pictogram (see p. 28). The pictophonograms composed of the signific "弓" usually refer to the bow and arrow. It's usually on the left side.

| 弯 | wān | curved, crooked | 弯曲 wānqū | winding |
| | | | 弯路 wānlù | crooked road |
| | | | 拐弯 guǎiwān | turn a corner |

| 弯 | | | | | | | | |
|---|---|---|---|---|---|---|---|---|
| | | | | | | | | |

| 强 | qiáng | strong, by foce | 强大 qiángdà | powerful |
| | | | 强壮 qiángzhuàng | strong |
| | | | 加强 jiāqiáng | strengthen |

| 强 | | | | | | | | |
|---|---|---|---|---|---|---|---|---|
| | | | | | | | | |

| 弹 | tán | shoot, elastic | 弹琴 tánqín | play the piano |
| | | | 弹力 tánlì | elastic force |
| | | | 弹性 tánxìng | elasticity |

| 弹 | | | | | | | | |
|---|---|---|---|---|---|---|---|---|
| | | | | | | | | |

# 【女部】

"女"象形字,三画,见 20 页。"女"作形旁的字多和女性有关。女字旁一般在字的左侧。

"女" is a 3 stroke pictogram (see p. 20). The pictophonograms composed of the signific "女" refer to the female sex. It's usually on the left side.

| 姐 | jie | elder sister | 姐姐 jiějie | elder sister |
| | | | 小姐 xiǎojiě | Miss |
| | | | 姐妹 jiěmèi | sisters |

| 姐 | | | | | | | | |
|---|---|---|---|---|---|---|---|---|
| | | | | | | | | |

| 妹 | mèi | younger sister | 妹妹 mèimei | younger sister |
| | | | 姐妹 jiěmèi | sisters |
| | | | 妹夫 mèifu | brother-in-law |

| 妹 | | | | | | | | |
|---|---|---|---|---|---|---|---|---|
| | | | | | | | | |

姑　　gū　　aunt

姑姑 gūgu　　aunt
姑娘 gūniang　girl
姑息 gūxī　　appease

| 姑 | | | | | | | | |
|---|---|---|---|---|---|---|---|---|

## 【小部】

"小"象形字,三画,见 14 页。"小"字旁有时写作"　"。
"小" is a 3 stroke pictogram (see p. 14). When used as a component, "小" is often written as "　".

少　　shǎo　　few, little

少量 shǎoliàng　a few
多少 duōshǎo　how many
减少 jiǎnshǎo　reduce

| 少 | | | | | | | | |
|---|---|---|---|---|---|---|---|---|

当　　dāng　　work as, equal

当然 dāngrán　of course
当面 dāngmiàn　to sb.'s face
当代 dāngdài　the present age

| 当 | | | | | | | | |
|---|---|---|---|---|---|---|---|---|

常　　cháng　　often, ordinary

常常 chángcháng　often
经常 jīngcháng　day-to-day
日常 rìcháng　daily

| 常 | | | | | | | | |
|---|---|---|---|---|---|---|---|---|

## 【子部】

"子"象形字,三画,见 9 页。"子"作形旁的字多和孩子有关。子字旁的位置比较灵活,在字的左侧时写作"孑"。
"子" is a 3 stroke pictogram (see p. 9). The pictophonograms composed of the signific "子" usually refer to children. Its position is flexible. When placed on the left side, "子" is written as "孑".

学　　xué　　study, learn

学习 xuéxí　　study
学生 xuéshēng　student
学校 xuéxiào　school

| 学 | | | | | | | | |
|---|---|---|---|---|---|---|---|---|

155

孙　　sūn　　grandson

孙子 sūnzi　　grandson
孙女 sūnnǚ　　granddaughter
子孙 zǐsūn　　descendants

| 孙 | | | | | | | | | |
|---|---|---|---|---|---|---|---|---|---|

## 【马部】

"马"象形字，三画，见 31 页。"马"作形旁的字大多和马有关。马字旁一般在字的左侧。

"马" is a 3 stroke pictogram (see p. 31). The pictophonograms composed of the signific "马" have to do with the horse. It's usually on the left side.

驾　　jià　　harness, drive

驾驶 jiàshǐ　　drive
驾驭 jiàyù　　drive, control
驾临 jiàlín　　your arrival

| 驾 | | | | | | | | | |
|---|---|---|---|---|---|---|---|---|---|

驶　　shǐ　　sail

驾驶 jiàshǐ　　drive
驶离 shǐlí　　pulled out
疾驶 jíshǐ　　speed by

| 驶 | | | | | | | | | |
|---|---|---|---|---|---|---|---|---|---|

## 【艹部】

"艹"像草形，偏旁部首，三画。"艹"旁的字和草本植物有关。艹字旁在字的上部。

"艹" looks like grass. It is a 3 stroke component. The pictophonograms composed of the signific "艹" refer to the herb. It's placed on the top.

花　　huā　　flower

鲜花 xiānhuā　　fresh flowers
花店 huādiàn　　florist
花生 huāshēng　　peanut

| 花 | | | | | | | | | |
|---|---|---|---|---|---|---|---|---|---|

菜　　cài　　vegetable

蔬菜 shūcài　　vegetable
菜单 càidān　　menu
菜刀 càidāo　　kitchen knife

| 菜 | | | | | | | | | |
|---|---|---|---|---|---|---|---|---|---|

茶　　　chá　　　tea

茶叶 cháyè　　tea
花茶 huāchá　scented tea
绿茶 lùchá　　green tea

| 茶 | | | | | | | | | |
|---|---|---|---|---|---|---|---|---|---|

【纟部】

"纟"是"糸"字的简写，三画，"糸"象形字，见 97 页。"纟"作形旁的字多和丝、线有关。偏旁"纟"在字的左侧。
"纟" has 3 stroke, it is simplified from "糸". "糸" is a pictogram (see p. 97). The pictophonograms composed of the signific "纟" refer to silk and thread. It's on the left side.

结　　　jié　　　tie, knot, form

结果 jiéguǒ　result
总结 zǒngjié　sum up
团结 tuánjié　unite

| 结 | | | | | | | | | |
|---|---|---|---|---|---|---|---|---|---|

经　　　jīng　　　warp, longitude

经济 jīngjì　　economy
经常 jīngcháng　day-to-day
已经 yǐjīng　　already

| 经 | | | | | | | | | |
|---|---|---|---|---|---|---|---|---|---|

给　　　gěi　　　give, for

送给 sònggěi　give
交给 jiāogěi　hand over
献给 xiàngěi　offer

| 给 | | | | | | | | | |
|---|---|---|---|---|---|---|---|---|---|

【辶部】

"辶"偏旁部首，三画。"辶"作形旁的字多和行走的意思有关。偏旁"辶"在字的左侧。
"辶" is a 3 stroke component. The pictophonograms composed of the signific "辶" usually refer to walking. It's on the left side.

过　　　guò　　　across, past

过去 guòqù　past
经过 jīngguò　go through
通过 tōngguò　traverse

| 过 | | | | | | | | | |
|---|---|---|---|---|---|---|---|---|---|

| 进 | jìn | advance, enter | 前进 qiánjìn | advance |
| | | | 进去 jìnqù | enter |
| | | | 请进 qǐngjìn | come in |

| 进 | | | | | | | | | |
|---|---|---|---|---|---|---|---|---|---|
| | | | | | | | | | |

| 远 | yuǎn | far, distant | 远方 yuǎnfāng | distant place |
| | | | 远道 yuǎndào | along way |
| | | | 远见 yuǎnjiàn | foresight |

| 远 | | | | | | | | | |
|---|---|---|---|---|---|---|---|---|---|
| | | | | | | | | | |

| 还 | huán | go back, give back | 还礼 huánlǐ | return a salute |
| | | | 还钱 huánqián | pay back |
| | | | 还价 huánjià | counter-offer |

| 还 | | | | | | | | | |
|---|---|---|---|---|---|---|---|---|---|
| | | | | | | | | | |

## 【王部】

"王"四画，代表两个象形字，一个是"王"字，见 24 页，一个是"玉"字，见 24 页。"王"作偏旁时有点变形。

" 王" is a 4 stroke component. It represents two pictograms. One is "王"(see p.24), the other is "玉" (see p.24). As component " 王" is out of shape a little.

| 现 | xiàn | present, appear | 现在 xiànzài | now |
| | | | 现代 xiàndài | modern times |
| | | | 现象 xiànxiàng | appearance |

| 现 | | | | | | | | | |
|---|---|---|---|---|---|---|---|---|---|
| | | | | | | | | | |

| 玩 | wán | play, amuse oneself | 玩具 wánjù | toy |
| | | | 好玩 hǎowán | amusing |
| | | | 玩笑 wánxiào | joke |

| 玩 | | | | | | | | | |
|---|---|---|---|---|---|---|---|---|---|
| | | | | | | | | | |

| 班 | bān | class, shift | 班长 bānzhǎng | class monitor |
| | | | 班机 bānjī | airliner |
| | | | 班车 bānchē | regular bus |

| 班 | | | | | | | | | |
|---|---|---|---|---|---|---|---|---|---|
| | | | | | | | | | |

# 【木部】

"木"象形字,四画,见 18 页。"木"作形旁的字都和树木、木材有关。木字旁的位置比较灵活,在左侧时写成瘦长形。

"木" is a 4 storke pictogram (see p. 18). The pictophongrams composed of the signific "木" refer to trees and wood. Its position is flexible. When placed on the left side, its form is long and thin.

**椅** yǐ　　chair

| 椅子 yǐzi | chair |
|---|---|
| 转椅 zhuànyǐ | swivel chair |
| 躺椅 tǎngyǐ | deck chair |

| 椅 | | | | | | | | | |
|---|---|---|---|---|---|---|---|---|---|

**桌** zhuō　　table, desk

| 桌子 zhuōzi | table |
|---|---|
| 书桌 shūzhuō | writing desk |
| 餐桌 cānzhuō | dining table |

| 桌 | | | | | | | | | |
|---|---|---|---|---|---|---|---|---|---|

**树** shù　　tree

| 树木 shùmù | trees |
|---|---|
| 树立 shùlì | set up |
| 树枝 shùzhī | branch |

| 树 | | | | | | | | | |
|---|---|---|---|---|---|---|---|---|---|

**杯** bēi　　cup

| 杯子 bēizi | cup |
|---|---|
| 茶杯 chábēi | teacup |
| 酒杯 jiǔbēi | glass |

| 杯 | | | | | | | | | |
|---|---|---|---|---|---|---|---|---|---|

**楼** lóu　　a storied building

| 楼房 lóufáng | building |
|---|---|
| 楼梯 lóutī | stairs |
| 楼道 lóudào | corridor |

| 楼 | | | | | | | | | |
|---|---|---|---|---|---|---|---|---|---|

**样** yàng　　appearance, sample

| 样子 yàngzi | appearance |
|---|---|
| 样品 yàngpǐn | specimen |
| 怎样 zěnyàng | how |

| 样 | | | | | | | | | |
|---|---|---|---|---|---|---|---|---|---|

# 【犬部】

"犬"象形字,本义指狗,四画。"犭"是"犬"字旁的变体,在字的左侧。犬字旁的字大多与狗或兽类有关。

"犬" is a 4 storke pictogram, meaning dog. The pictophonograms composed of the signific "犬" refer to animals like the dog. When placed on the left side, "犬" is written as "犭".

哭     kū     cry, weep

大哭 dà kū   cry loudly
痛哭 tòngkū   cry bitterly
哭泣 kūqì   cry, weep

| 哭 | | | | | | | | | |
|---|---|---|---|---|---|---|---|---|---|

狗     gǒu     dog

狗皮 gǒupí   dogskin
母狗 mǔgǒu   bitch
狗熊 gǒuxióng   black bear

| 狗 | | | | | | | | | |
|---|---|---|---|---|---|---|---|---|---|

狼     láng     wolf

豺狼 cháiláng   wolf
狼狗 lánggǒu   wolfhound
狼牙 lángyá   wolf's fang

| 狼 | | | | | | | | | |
|---|---|---|---|---|---|---|---|---|---|

# 【歹部】

"歹"象形字,四画。古"歹"字像一块死人的残骨,"歹"作形旁的字多与死亡有关。

"歹" is a 4 stroke pictogram. The ancient form of "歹" depicts a bone of a dead person. The pictophonograms composed of the signific "歹" have to do with death.

死     sǐ     die

死人 sǐrén   the dead
死亡 sǐwáng   death
死活 sǐhuó   life or death

| 死 | | | | | | | | | |
|---|---|---|---|---|---|---|---|---|---|

残     cán     injure, incomplete

残废 cánfèi   maimed
残杀 cánshā   murder
残暴 cánbào   ruthless

| 残 | | | | | | | | | |
|---|---|---|---|---|---|---|---|---|---|

列     liè            arrange

排列 páiliè     arrange
列举 lièjǔ     enumerate
列车 lièchē     train

| 列 | | | | | | | | | |
|---|---|---|---|---|---|---|---|---|---|

## 【车部】

"车"象形字，四画，见30页。"车"作形旁的字大多和车有关。车字旁一般在字的左侧。

"车" is a 4 stroke pictogram (see p. 30). The pictophonograms composed of the signific "车" relate to vehicles. It's usually on the left side.

转     zhuàn        turn

转动 zhuàndòng     turn
旋转 xuánzhuàn     revolve
转速 zhuànsù     rotational speed

| 转 | | | | | | | | | |
|---|---|---|---|---|---|---|---|---|---|

轻     qīng         light

轻便 qīngbiàn     light
轻松 qīngsōng     relaxed
年轻 niánqīng     young

| 轻 | | | | | | | | | |
|---|---|---|---|---|---|---|---|---|---|

较     jiào         compare

较量 jiàoliàng     have a contest
比较 bǐjiào     compare
较好 jiàohǎo     fairly good

| 较 | | | | | | | | | |
|---|---|---|---|---|---|---|---|---|---|

## 【戈部】

"戈"象形字，四画。古代"戈"字像一种兵器。"戈"作形旁的字有的和武器、战争有关。戈字旁一般在字的右侧。

"戈" is a 4 stroke pictogram. The ancient form of "戈" depicts an arm. The pictophonograms composed of the signific "戈" refer to arms and war. It's usually on the right side.

我     wǒ          I

我们 wǒmen     we
自我 zìwǒ     self
我方 wǒfāng     our side

| 我 | | | | | | | | | |
|---|---|---|---|---|---|---|---|---|---|

或     huò     or, perhaps

或者 huòzhě    or
或许 huòxǔ    perhaps
或然 huòrán    probable

| 或 | | | | | | | | | |
|---|---|---|---|---|---|---|---|---|---|

划     huà     delimit, draw

规划 guīhuà    plan
谋划 móuhuà    scheme
划分 huàfēn    divide

| 划 | | | | | | | | | |
|---|---|---|---|---|---|---|---|---|---|

# 【攵部】

"攵"偏旁部首,四画。"攵"作形旁的字有的和手的动作有关。"攵"一般在字的右侧。

"攵" is a 4 stroke component. Some pictophonograms composed of the signific "攵" refer to the movement of the hand. It's ususally on the right side.

救     jiù     rescue, save

救命 jiùmìng    save sb.'s life
救护 jiùhù    give first-aid
抢救 qiǎngjiù    rescue

| 救 | | | | | | | | | |
|---|---|---|---|---|---|---|---|---|---|

教     jiào     teach

教学 jiàoxué    teaching
教师 jiàoshī    teacher
教室 jiàoshì    classroom

| 教 | | | | | | | | | |
|---|---|---|---|---|---|---|---|---|---|

收     shōu     receive

收到 shōudào    receive
丰收 fēngshōu    bumper harvest
收入 shōurù    income

| 收 | | | | | | | | | |
|---|---|---|---|---|---|---|---|---|---|

故     gù     former, reason

故事 gùshi    story
故宫 gùgōng    the Imperial Palace
故乡 gùxiāng    native place

| 故 | | | | | | | | | |
|---|---|---|---|---|---|---|---|---|---|

# 【日部】

"日"象形字，四画，见12页。"日"作形旁的字多和太阳有关。日字旁的位置比较灵活。

"日" is a 4 stroke pictogram (see p. 12). The pictophonograms composed of the signific "日" relate to the sun. Its position is flexible.

时　　shí　　time

| 时间 | shíjiān | time |
| 时候 | shíhou | moment |
| 时代 | shídài | fairly good |

| 时 | | | | | | | | | |
|---|---|---|---|---|---|---|---|---|---|

星　　xīng　　star, heavenly body

| 星球 | xīngqiú | heavenly body |
| 星期 | xīngqī | week |
| 明星 | míngxīng | star |

| 星 | | | | | | | | | |
|---|---|---|---|---|---|---|---|---|---|

晚　　wǎn　　evening, night

| 晚上 | wǎnshang | evening |
| 晚饭 | wǎnfàn | supper |
| 今晚 | jīnwǎn | this evening |

| 晚 | | | | | | | | | |
|---|---|---|---|---|---|---|---|---|---|

春　　chūn　　spring

| 春天 | chūntiān | spring |
| 春季 | chūnjì | spring |
| 青春 | qīngchūn | youth |

| 春 | | | | | | | | | |
|---|---|---|---|---|---|---|---|---|---|

晴　　qíng　　fine, clear

| 晴天 | qíngtiān | fine day |
| 晴朗 | qínglǎng | sunny |
| 晴空 | qíngkōng | clear sky |

| 晴 | | | | | | | | | |
|---|---|---|---|---|---|---|---|---|---|

暖　　nuǎn　　warm

| 暖和 | nuǎnhuo | warm |
| 温暖 | wēnnuǎn | warm |
| 暖气 | nuǎnqì | central heating |

| 暖 | | | | | | | | | |
|---|---|---|---|---|---|---|---|---|---|

# 【贝部】

"贝"象形字,四画,见 33 页。"贝"作形旁的字大多和钱财、交易有关。贝字旁的位置比较灵活,在左侧时写成瘦长形。

"贝" is a 4 stroke pictogram (see p. 33). The pictophonograms composed of the signific "贝" refer to wealth and money. Its position is flexible. When placed on the left side, its form is long and thin.

货  huò  goods

货币 huòbì　money
货物 huòwù　goods
货车 huòchē　goods train

| 货 | | | | | | | | | |
|---|---|---|---|---|---|---|---|---|---|

贵  guì  expensive, costly

贵重 guìzhòng　valuable
昂贵 ángguì　expensive
贵宾 guìbīn　honoured guest

| 贵 | | | | | | | | | |
|---|---|---|---|---|---|---|---|---|---|

费  fèi  fee, charge

费用 fèiyòng　cost
学费 xuéfèi　tuition fees
免费 miǎnfèi　free of charge

| 费 | | | | | | | | | |
|---|---|---|---|---|---|---|---|---|---|

# 【见部】

"见"会意字,四画,见 81 页。"见"作形旁的字多与观看有关。见字旁的位置比较灵活。

"见" is a 4 stroke associative character (see p. 81). The pictophonograms composed of the signific "见" have to do with watching and seeing. Its position is flexible.

观  guān  look at, watch

参观 cānguān　visit
观看 guānkàn　watch
观众 guānzhòng　spectator

| 观 | | | | | | | | | |
|---|---|---|---|---|---|---|---|---|---|

览  lǎn  look at, see

展览 zhǎnlǎn　exhibit
博览 bólǎn　read extensively
游览 yóulǎn　tour

| 览 | | | | | | | | | |
|---|---|---|---|---|---|---|---|---|---|

觉　　　jué　　　sense

視觉 shìjué　　visual sense
感觉 gǎnjué　　sensation
觉得 juéde　　feel

| 觉 | | | | | | | | | | |
|---|---|---|---|---|---|---|---|---|---|---|

## 【牛部】

"牛"象形字,四画,见 26 页。"牛"作形旁的字和牛有关。牛字旁在左侧时写法有点变形。

"牛" is a 4 stroke pictogram (see p. 26). The pictophonograms composed of the signific "牛" refer to the ox. When placed on the left side, it's out of shape a little.

牧　　　mù　　　herd, tend

放牧 fàngmù　　herd
牧业 mùyè　　stock raising
牧场 mùchǎng　　grazing land

| 牧 | | | | | | | | | | |
|---|---|---|---|---|---|---|---|---|---|---|

物　　　wù　　　thing

动物 dòngwù　　animal
生物 shēngwù　　living things
事物 shìwù　　object

| 物 | | | | | | | | | | |
|---|---|---|---|---|---|---|---|---|---|---|

特　　　tè　　　special

特别 tèbié　　special
特点 tèdiǎn　　characteristic
特殊 tèshū　　particular

| 特 | | | | | | | | | | |
|---|---|---|---|---|---|---|---|---|---|---|

## 【手部】

"手"象形字,四画,见 25 页。"手"作形旁的字都和手或手的动作有关。手字旁在左侧时写成"扌"。

"手" is a 4 stroke pictogram, (see p. 25). The pictophonograms composed of the signific "手" have to do with the to hand. When placed on the left side, it's written as "扌".

掌　　　zhǎng　　　palm

手掌 shǒuzhǎng　　palm
掌声 zhǎngshēng　　applause
掌握 zhǎngwò　　grasp

| 掌 | | | | | | | | | | |
|---|---|---|---|---|---|---|---|---|---|---|

打      dǎ      strike, hit, play

| 打开 dǎkāi | open |
| 打扫 dǎsǎo | sweep |
| 打架 dǎjià | come to blows |

| 打 | | | | | | | | | |
|---|---|---|---|---|---|---|---|---|---|

提      tí      carry, lift, bring up

| 提高 tígāo | raise |
| 提问 tíwèn | put questions to |
| 提前 tíqián | advance |

| 提 | | | | | | | | | |
|---|---|---|---|---|---|---|---|---|---|

挂      guà      put up, hang

| 挂图 guàtú | wall map |
| 挂号 guàhào | register |
| 挂念 guàniàn | miss |

| 挂 | | | | | | | | | |
|---|---|---|---|---|---|---|---|---|---|

接      jiē      receive, catch, join

| 接见 jiējiàn | receive sb. |
| 接受 jiēshòu | accept |
| 接通 jiētōng | put through |

| 接 | | | | | | | | | |
|---|---|---|---|---|---|---|---|---|---|

推      tuī      push

| 推动 tuīdòng | push forward |
| 推进 tuījìn | push on |
| 推广 tuīguǎng | popularize |

| 推 | | | | | | | | | |
|---|---|---|---|---|---|---|---|---|---|

找      zhǎo      look for

| 寻找 xúnzhǎo | look for |
| 找钱 zhǎoqián | give change |
| 找事 zhǎoshì | look for a job |

| 找 | | | | | | | | | |
|---|---|---|---|---|---|---|---|---|---|

报      bào      report

| 报告 bàogào | report |
| 报纸 bàozhǐ | newspaper |
| 报道 bàodào | news report |

| 报 | | | | | | | | | |
|---|---|---|---|---|---|---|---|---|---|

# 【片部】

"片"指事字，四画，见 53 页。"片"作形旁的字大多和木或竹等片状物体有关。片字旁一般在字的左侧。

"片" is a 4 stroke indicative character (see p.53).
The pictophonograms composed of the signific "片" refer to wood or bombo objects which have a slice form. It's on the left side.

牌　pái　plate, brand, cards

牌子 páizi　plate
门牌 ménpái　doorplate
车牌 chēpái　number plate

| 牌 | | | | | | | | |
|---|---|---|---|---|---|---|---|---|

版　bǎn　printing plate

出版 chūbǎn　publish
版本 bǎnběn　edition
版权 bǎnquán　copyright

| 版 | | | | | | | | |
|---|---|---|---|---|---|---|---|---|

# 【斤部】

"斤"象形字，四画，见 23 页。斤作形旁的字大多与斧子、砍折的意思有关。斤字旁的位置比较灵活。

"斤" is a 4 stroke pictogram (see p.23). The pictophonograms composed of the signific "斤" relate to the axe or chopping. Its position is flexible.

断　duàn　break, snap

切断 qiēduàn　cut off
不断 búduàn　unceasing
断交 duànjiāo　break off a friendship

| 断 | | | | | | | | |
|---|---|---|---|---|---|---|---|---|

新　xīn　new

新年 xīnnián　New Year
新闻 xīnwén　news
新鲜 xīnxiān　fresh

| 新 | | | | | | | | |
|---|---|---|---|---|---|---|---|---|

所　suǒ　place

场所 chǎngsuǒ　place
所以 suǒyǐ　so, therefore
所有 suǒyǒu　own, possess

| 所 | | | | | | | | |
|---|---|---|---|---|---|---|---|---|

167

# 【爪部】

"爪"象形字，四画，见 23 页。爪作形旁的字大多和手、爪有关。"爪"字作偏旁有一个变体，写作" "。

"爪" is a 4 stroke pictogram (see p.23). The pictophongrams composed of the signific "爪" refer to the hand and claw. When used as an element, "爪" is written as" ".

## 爱

ài love

| 爱 | | | | | | | | | |
|---|---|---|---|---|---|---|---|---|---|

爱情 àiqíng love
爱人 àirén husband or wife
热爱 rèài ardently love

## 受

shòu receive, bear

| 受 | | | | | | | | | |
|---|---|---|---|---|---|---|---|---|---|

接受 jiēshòu accept
忍受 rěnshòu bear
享受 xiǎngshòu enjoy

## 妥

tuǒ appropriate

| 妥 | | | | | | | | | |
|---|---|---|---|---|---|---|---|---|---|

妥当 tuǒdàng appropriate
妥善 tuǒshàn proper
稳妥 wěntuǒ safe

# 【父部】

"父"象形字，四画，见 27 页。"父"作形旁的字大多表示男性长辈。父字旁在字的上部，位置比较固定。

"父" is a 4 stroke pictogram (see p.27). The pictophongrams composed of the signific "父" refer to male elders . It's placed on the top.

## 爹

diē father

| 爹 | | | | | | | | | |
|---|---|---|---|---|---|---|---|---|---|

爹爹 diēdie dad
爹娘 diēniáng mum and dad

## 爷

yé grandfather

| 爷 | | | | | | | | | |
|---|---|---|---|---|---|---|---|---|---|

爷爷 yéye grandfather
老爷 lǎoye sir, master
少爷 shàoye young master

# 【月部】

"月"作偏旁代表两个象形字,一是月亮的"月"字,见13页,一是"肉"字,见45页。因此,"月"字作形旁的字,有的和月亮有关。有的和人体有关。月亮的"月",一般在字的右方,"肉月"一般在字左方。

The element "月" represents two pictograms. One is "月" (see p. 13), and the other is "肉" (see p. 45). The pictophonograms composed of the signific "月" relate to the moon, and those of the signific "肉" relate to the body. The component "月" is on the right side, and the component "肉" is on the left side.

| 朗 | lǎng | clear, bright | 晴朗 qínglǎng | clear and bright |
| | | | 明朗 mínglǎng | clear |
| | | | 朗诵 lǎngsòng | recite |

| 朗 | | | | | | | | | | |
|---|---|---|---|---|---|---|---|---|---|---|

| 服 | fú | clothes | 衣服 yīfu | clothes |
| | | | 服装 fúzhuāng | dress |
| | | | 服务 fúwù | serve |

| 服 | | | | | | | | | | |
|---|---|---|---|---|---|---|---|---|---|---|

| 肚 | dù | belly | 肚子 dùzi | belly |
| | | | 肚脐 dùqí | navel |
| | | | 肚皮 dùpí | belly |

| 肚 | | | | | | | | | | |
|---|---|---|---|---|---|---|---|---|---|---|

| 脚 | jiǎo | foot | 脚步 jiǎobù | step, pace |
| | | | 脚跟 jiǎogēn | heel |
| | | | 墙脚 qiángjiǎo | the foot of a wall |

| 脚 | | | | | | | | | | |
|---|---|---|---|---|---|---|---|---|---|---|

| 脑 | nǎo | brain | 大脑 dànǎo | cerebrum |
| | | | 脑子 nǎozi | brain |
| | | | 电脑 diànnǎo | computer |

| 脑 | | | | | | | | | | |
|---|---|---|---|---|---|---|---|---|---|---|

| 脏 | zàng | internal organs | 心脏 xīnzàng | heart |
| | | | 肝脏 gānzàng | liver |
| | | | 肾脏 shènzàng | kidneys |

| 脏 | | | | | | | | | | |
|---|---|---|---|---|---|---|---|---|---|---|

朋　péng　friend

朋友 péngyou　friend
朋党 péngdǎng　clique
良朋 liángpéng　good friend

| 朋 | | | | | | | | | |
|---|---|---|---|---|---|---|---|---|---|

## 【欠部】

"欠"象形字,四画,见41页。"欠"字作形旁的字多和嘴出气有关。欠字旁的位置一般在右侧。
"欠" is a 4 stroke pictogram (see p.41). The pictophongrams composed of the significant "欠" relate to exhalation. It's on the right side.

歇　xiē　have a rest

歇息 xiēxi　have a rest
歇工 xiēgōng　stop work
歇凉 xiēliáng　relax in a cool place

| 歇 | | | | | | | | | |
|---|---|---|---|---|---|---|---|---|---|

歉　qiàn　apology

道歉 dàoqiàn　offer an apology
抱歉 bàoqiàn　be sorry
歉意 qiànyì　apology

| 歉 | | | | | | | | | |
|---|---|---|---|---|---|---|---|---|---|

欧　oū　short of Europe

欧洲 Oūzhōu　Europe
西欧 Xī'ōu　Western Europe
东欧 Dōng'ōu　Eastern Europe

| 欧 | | | | | | | | | |
|---|---|---|---|---|---|---|---|---|---|

## 【火部】

"火"象形字,四画,见29页。"火"作形旁的字大多和火有关。火字旁一般在左侧。"灬"是"火"的变体,作偏旁在字的下部。
"火" is a 4 stroke pictogram (see p.29). The pictophongrams composed of the significant "火" relate to fire. It's on the left side. When placed on the bottom, it's written as "灬".

灯　dēng　lamp, lantern

电灯 diàndēng　electric light
油灯 yóudēng　oil lamp
宫灯 gōngdēng　palace lantern

| 灯 | | | | | | | | | |
|---|---|---|---|---|---|---|---|---|---|

烧    shāo    burn

烧火 shāohuǒ make a fire
烧香 shāoxiāng burn joss sticks
燃烧 ránshāo burn

| 烧 | | | | | | | | | |
|---|---|---|---|---|---|---|---|---|---|

热    rè    heat, hot

热水 rèshuǐ hot water
热爱 rèài ardently love
热情 rèqíng enthusiasm

| 热 | | | | | | | | | |
|---|---|---|---|---|---|---|---|---|---|

点    diǎn    to light, spot, point

点火 diǎnhuǒ light a fire
点燃 diǎnrán kindle
特点 tèdiǎn characteristic

| 点 | | | | | | | | | |
|---|---|---|---|---|---|---|---|---|---|

然    rán    so, like that

然后 ránhòu then
当然 dāngrán of course
虽然 suīrán though

| 然 | | | | | | | | | |
|---|---|---|---|---|---|---|---|---|---|

# 【户部】

"户"象形字,四画,见15页。户字作形旁的字多和门户有关。户字旁的位置比较固定。

"户" is a 4 stroke pictogram (see p. 15). The pictophongrams composed of the signific "户" relate to the door. Its position is fixed.

扇    shàn    leaf, fan

门扇 ménshàn door leaf
扇子 shànzi fan
电扇 diànshàn electric fan

| 扇 | | | | | | | | | |
|---|---|---|---|---|---|---|---|---|---|

启    qǐ    open, enlighten

启程 qǐchéng set out
启发 qǐfā arouse
启蒙 qǐméng initiate

| 启 | | | | | | | | | |
|---|---|---|---|---|---|---|---|---|---|

雇　　gù　　hire, employ

雇工 gùgōng　hire labour
雇佣 gùyōng　employ
解雇 jiěgù　discharge

| 雇 | | | | | | | | | |
|---|---|---|---|---|---|---|---|---|---|

## 【心部】

"心"象形字，四画，见 29 页。"心"字作形旁的字大多和心理活动有关。心字旁一般在字的下侧。心字旁在左侧写作"忄"。
"心" is a 4 stroke pictogram (see p. 29). The pictophongrams composed of the signific "心" relate to mental action. It's usually placed at the bottom. When placed on the left side, it's written as "忄".

思　　si　　think

思想 sīxiǎng　thought
思念 sīniàn　think of
思考 sīkǎo　think deeply

| 思 | | | | | | | | | |
|---|---|---|---|---|---|---|---|---|---|

感　　gǎn　　sense, feel

感动 gǎndòng　move
感想 gǎnxiǎng　impressions
感谢 gǎnxiè　thank

| 感 | | | | | | | | | |
|---|---|---|---|---|---|---|---|---|---|

意　　yì　　meaning, idea

意思 yìsi　meaning
意义 yìyi　significance
意见 yìjiàn　idea, opinion

| 意 | | | | | | | | | |
|---|---|---|---|---|---|---|---|---|---|

惯　　guàn　　be in the habit of

习惯 xíguàn　habit
惯例 guànlì　convention
惯性 guànxìng　inertia

| 惯 | | | | | | | | | |
|---|---|---|---|---|---|---|---|---|---|

快　　kuài　　pleased, fast

快乐 kuàilè　happy
快活 kuàihuó　cheerful
快车 kuàichē　express train

| 快 | | | | | | | | | |
|---|---|---|---|---|---|---|---|---|---|

慢　　màn　　slow, supercilious

慢车 mànchē　　slow train
慢走 mànzǒu　　don't go yet; good-bye
傲慢 àomàn　　arrogant

| 慢 | | | | | | | | | |
|---|---|---|---|---|---|---|---|---|---|

## 【水部】

"水"象形字，四画，见 14 页。"水"字作形旁的字大多和水或液体有关。水字旁在左侧时写作"氵"。

"水" is a 4 stroke pictogram (see p. 14). The pictophongrams composed of the signific "水" relate to water. When placed on the left side, "水" is written as "氵".

江　　jiāng　　river

长江 chángjiāng　　Changjiang River
江山 jiāngshān　　landscape
江南 jiāngnán　　south of Changjiang

| 江 | | | | | | | | | |
|---|---|---|---|---|---|---|---|---|---|

海　　hǎi　　sea

大海 dàhǎi　　sea
海军 hǎijūn　　navy
上海 Shànghǎi　　Shanghai

| 海 | | | | | | | | | |
|---|---|---|---|---|---|---|---|---|---|

洗　　xǐ　　wash

洗手 xǐshǒu　　wash the hands
洗头 xǐtóu　　wash the hair
洗澡 xǐzǎo　　have a bath

| 洗 | | | | | | | | | |
|---|---|---|---|---|---|---|---|---|---|

活　　huó　　live

生活 shēnghuó　　life
活动 huódòng　　move about
活跃 huóyuè　　brisk

| 活 | | | | | | | | | |
|---|---|---|---|---|---|---|---|---|---|

法　　fǎ　　law, method

法律 fǎlǜ　　law
方法 fāngfǎ　　method
办法 bànfǎ　　way, means

| 法 | | | | | | | | | |
|---|---|---|---|---|---|---|---|---|---|

# 【示部】

"示"象形字,五画,见 21 页。"示"字作形旁的字多和祭祀、鬼神、祸福有关。示字旁在左侧时写作"礻"。

"示" is a 5 stroke pictogram (see p.21). The pictophongrams composed of the signific "示" refer to sacrifices, gods and misfortune. When placed on the left side, the element "示" is written as "礻".

祭    jì      offer a sacrifice to

祭祀 jìsì   offer sacrifices to
祭典 jìdiǎn   hold a memorial ceremony
祭文 jìwén   funeral oration

| 祭 | | | | | | | | |
|---|---|---|---|---|---|---|---|---|

祝    zhù      wish

祝贺 zhùhè   congratulate
祝福 zhùfú   blessing
庆祝 qìngzhù   celebrate

| 祝 | | | | | | | | |
|---|---|---|---|---|---|---|---|---|

福    fú      good fortune

幸福 xìngfú   happiness
福气 fúqì   happy lot
福利 fúlì   welfare

| 福 | | | | | | | | |
|---|---|---|---|---|---|---|---|---|

祖    zǔ      ancestor

祖父 zǔfù   grandfather
祖母 zǔmǔ   grandmother
祖国 zǔguó   homeland

| 祖 | | | | | | | | |
|---|---|---|---|---|---|---|---|---|

# 【石部】

"石"象形字,五画,见 10 页。石字作形旁的字多和石头有关。石字旁一般在字的左侧。

"石" is a 5 stroke pictogram (see p.10). The pictophongrams composed of the signific "石" relate to stone. It's on the left side.

碗    wǎn      bowl

饭碗 fànwǎn   bowl
瓷碗 cíwǎn   china bowl
碗筷 wǎnkuài   bowls and chopsticks

| 碗 | | | | | | | | |
|---|---|---|---|---|---|---|---|---|

硬　yìng　strong, hard

坚硬　jiānyìng　hard, solid
硬度　yìngdù　hardness
硬币　yìngbì　coin

| 硬 | | | | | | | | |
|---|---|---|---|---|---|---|---|---|

砖　zhuān　brick

砖头　zhuāntóu　brick
砖厂　zhuānchǎng　brickfield
砖茶　zhuānchá　brick tea

| 砖 | | | | | | | | |
|---|---|---|---|---|---|---|---|---|

# 【目部】

"目"象形字，五画，37 页。"目"字作形旁的字多和眼睛有关。目字旁多在左侧。

"目" is a 5 stroke pictogram (see p. 37). The pictophongrams composed of the significant "目" relate to eyes. It's on the left side.

眼　yǎn　eye

眼睛　yǎnjīng　eye
眼镜　yǎnjìng　glasses
眼科　yǎnkē　ophthalmology

| 眼 | | | | | | | | |
|---|---|---|---|---|---|---|---|---|

睛　jīng　eyeball

眼睛　yǎnjīng　eye
目不转睛　　gaze fixedly
mùbù zhuǎn jīng

| 睛 | | | | | | | | |
|---|---|---|---|---|---|---|---|---|

瞎　xiā　blind

瞎子　xiāzi　blind
瞎说　xiāshuō　talk rubbish
瞎话　xiāhuà　untruth

| 瞎 | | | | | | | | |
|---|---|---|---|---|---|---|---|---|

瞧　qiáo　look

瞧见　qiáojiàn　see
瞧病　qiáobìng　see a doctor
瞧瞧　qiáoqiao　look

| 瞧 | | | | | | | | |
|---|---|---|---|---|---|---|---|---|

# 【田部】

"田"象形字，五画，见 34 页。田字作形旁的字多和田地、耕作有关。田字旁的位置比较灵活。

"田" is a 5 stroke pictogram (see p. 34). The pictophongrams composed of the signific "田" relate to fields and tillage. Its position is flexible.

## 畜

xù　　raise

畜牧　xùmù　　raise livestock
畜产　xùchǎn　livestock
畜养　xùyǎng　raise

| 畜 | | | | | | | | | |
|---|---|---|---|---|---|---|---|---|---|

## 留

liú　　stay, remain

留学　liúxué　　study abroad
留念　liúniàn　accept as a souvenir
居留　jūliú　　reside

| 留 | | | | | | | | | |
|---|---|---|---|---|---|---|---|---|---|

## 累

lèi　　tired

劳累　láolèi　　tired
累活　lèihuó　tiring work
连累　liánlèi　implicate

| 累 | | | | | | | | | |
|---|---|---|---|---|---|---|---|---|---|

# 【矢部】

"矢"象形字，五画。古代"矢"字像一支箭。矢字作形旁的字多和箭有关。矢字旁一般在左侧。

"矢" is a 5 stroke pictogram. The ancient form of "矢" depicts an arrow. The pictophongrams composed of the signific "矢" relate to the arrow. It's on the left side.

## 短

duǎn　　short

短期　duǎnqī　　short-term
短小　duǎnxiǎo　short and small
长短　chángduǎn　length

| 短 | | | | | | | | | |
|---|---|---|---|---|---|---|---|---|---|

## 知

zhī　　know

知道　zhīdào　　know
知识　zhīshi　knowledge
知心　zhīxīn　intimate

| 知 | | | | | | | | | |
|---|---|---|---|---|---|---|---|---|---|

矮　ǎi　short(of stature), low

矮小　ǎixiǎo　short and small
矮子　ǎizi　dwarf
高矮　gāoǎi　height

| 矮 | | | | | | | | | |
|---|---|---|---|---|---|---|---|---|---|

## 【禾部】

"禾"象形字,五画,见 19 页。"禾"字作形旁的字多和粮食作物或农业有关。禾字旁多在字的左侧。

"禾" is a 5 stroke pictogram (see p. 19). The pictophongrams composed of the signific "禾" relate to crops or agriculture. It's usually placed on the left side.

季　jì　season

季节　jìjié　season
春季　chūnjì　spring
雨季　yǔjì　rainy season

| 季 | | | | | | | | | |
|---|---|---|---|---|---|---|---|---|---|

和　hé　gentle, and

和风　héfēng　soft breeze
和平　hépíng　peace
和气　héqi　gentle

| 和 | | | | | | | | | |
|---|---|---|---|---|---|---|---|---|---|

积　jī　amass

积压　jīyā　keep long in stock
积累　jīlěi　accumulate
积极　jījí　active

| 积 | | | | | | | | | |
|---|---|---|---|---|---|---|---|---|---|

## 【白部】

"白"象形字,五画,见 12 页。"白"字作形旁的字多和白色、明亮有关。白字旁的位置较灵活。

"白" is a 5 stroke pictogram (see p. 12). The pictophongrams composed of the signific "白" relate to white colour or light. Its position is flexible.

泉　quán　spring

泉水　quánshuǐ　spring
矿泉　kuàngquán　mineral spring
源泉　yuánquán　source

| 泉 | | | | | | | | | |
|---|---|---|---|---|---|---|---|---|---|

**的**     de     (auxiliary word)

| | | |
|---|---|---|
| 我的 | wǒde | my |
| 你的 | nǐde | your |
| 他的 | tāde | his |

| 的 | | | | | | | | | | | |
|---|---|---|---|---|---|---|---|---|---|---|---|

**百**     bǎi     hundred

| | | |
|---|---|---|
| 一百 | yībǎi | one hundred |
| 百万 | bǎiwàn | million |
| 百年 | bǎinián | a hundred years |

| 百 | | | | | | | | | | | |
|---|---|---|---|---|---|---|---|---|---|---|---|

## 【疒部】

偏旁部首,"疒"五画。"疒"作形旁的字多和疾病有关。疒字旁的位置比较固定。

"疒" is a 5 stroke component. The pictophonograms composed of the signific "疒" relate to disease. Its position is fixed.

**疼**     téng     ache, pain

| | | |
|---|---|---|
| 疼痛 | téngtòng | pain |
| 头疼 | tóuténg | have a headache |
| 心疼 | xīnténg | love dearly |

| 疼 | | | | | | | | | | | |
|---|---|---|---|---|---|---|---|---|---|---|---|

**痛**     tòng     ache, pain

| | | |
|---|---|---|
| 痛苦 | tòngkǔ | pain |
| 痛心 | tòngxīn | distressed |
| 悲痛 | bēitòng | deep sorrow |

| 痛 | | | | | | | | | | | |
|---|---|---|---|---|---|---|---|---|---|---|---|

**疾**     jí     disease

| | | |
|---|---|---|
| 疾病 | jíbìng | disease |
| 疾苦 | jíkǔ | sufferings |
| 残疾 | cánjī | deformity |

| 疾 | | | | | | | | | | | |
|---|---|---|---|---|---|---|---|---|---|---|---|

**瘦**     shòu     thin, lean

| | | |
|---|---|---|
| 瘦弱 | shòuruò | thin and weak |
| 瘦小 | shòuxiǎo | thin and small |
| 瘦子 | shòuzi | a lean person |

| 瘦 | | | | | | | | | | | |
|---|---|---|---|---|---|---|---|---|---|---|---|

# 【立部】

"立"象形字,五画,见 7 页。"立"作形旁的字多与站立有关。
立字旁的位置比较灵活。在左侧时写法有点变形。

"立" is a 5 stroke pictogram (see p. 7). The pictophongrams composed of the significant "立" relate to standing. Its position is flexible. When placed on the left side, the element "立" is out of shape a little.

## 竖

shù     vertical, stand

竖立 shùlì    erect
横竖 héngshù   anyway
竖起 shùqǐ    erect

| 竖 | | | | | | | | | |
|---|---|---|---|---|---|---|---|---|---|

## 童

tóng     child

儿童 értóng    child
童年 tóngnián   childhood
童话 tónghuà   children's stories

| 童 | | | | | | | | | |
|---|---|---|---|---|---|---|---|---|---|

## 亲

qīn     parent, close, kiss

父亲 fùqin    father
母亲 mǔqin    mother
亲人 qīnrén   one's family members

| 亲 | | | | | | | | | |
|---|---|---|---|---|---|---|---|---|---|

# 【穴部】

"穴"即洞穴,五画。"穴"字作形旁的字多和洞穴有关。穴字旁在字的上部。

"穴" means hole, it has 5 stroke. The pictophongrams composed of the significant "穴" relate to holes. It's placed on the top.

## 窗

chuāng     window

窗户 chuānghu    window
窗口 chuāngkǒu   wicket
窗台 chuāngtái   windowsill

| 窗 | | | | | | | | | |
|---|---|---|---|---|---|---|---|---|---|

## 容

róng     hold, looks

容器 róngqì    container
容易 róngyì    easy
笑容 xiàoróng   a smiling face

| 容 | | | | | | | | | |
|---|---|---|---|---|---|---|---|---|---|

穿　chuān　penetrate, wear

穿过 chuānguò　pass through
穿戴 chuāndài　dress
看穿 kànchuān　see through

| 穿 | | | | | | | | | | |
|---|---|---|---|---|---|---|---|---|---|---|

## 【耳部】

"耳"象形字,六画,见 40 页。"耳"作形旁的字多和耳朵有关。耳字旁的位置比较灵活。
"耳" is a 6 stroke pictogram (see p. 40). · The pictophongrams composed of the signific "耳" relate to the ear. Its position is flexible.

闻　wén　hear, news

新闻 xīnwén　news
耳闻 ěrwén　hear
闻名 wénmíng　famous

| 闻 | | | | | | | | | | |
|---|---|---|---|---|---|---|---|---|---|---|

聪　cōng　acute hearing

聪明 cōngmíng　intelligent
聪慧 cōnghuì　bright
聪颖 cōngyíng　intelligent

| 聪 | | | | | | | | | | |
|---|---|---|---|---|---|---|---|---|---|---|

职　zhí　duty, job, post

职业 zhíyè　profession
职员 zhíyuán　office worker
职务 zhíwù　post, duties

| 职 | | | | | | | | | | |
|---|---|---|---|---|---|---|---|---|---|---|

## 【页部】

"页"象形字,六画,见 33 页。"页"字作形旁的字多和头、颈有关。页字旁一般在字的右侧。
"页" is a 6 stroke pictogram (see p. 33). The pictophongrams composed of the signific "页" relate to the head and neck. It's on the right side.

顾　gù　look at, attend to

照顾 zhàogù　look after
顾虑 gùlù　misgiving
顾问 gùwèn　adviser

| 顾 | | | | | | | | | | |
|---|---|---|---|---|---|---|---|---|---|---|

| 题 | tí | title, subject | 题目 tímù title |
| | | | 问题 wèntí question |
| | | | 话题 huàtí subject of conversation |

| 题 | | | | | | | | | |
|---|---|---|---|---|---|---|---|---|---|

| 预 | yù | in advance | 预备 yùbèi prepare |
| | | | 预订 yùdìng subscribe |
| | | | 预报 yùbào forecast |

| 预 | | | | | | | | | |
|---|---|---|---|---|---|---|---|---|---|

| 领 | lǐng | neck, collar, lead | 领子 lǐngzi collar |
| | | | 领导 lǐngdǎo lead |
| | | | 带领 dàilǐng guide |

| 领 | | | | | | | | | |
|---|---|---|---|---|---|---|---|---|---|

## 【虫部】

"虫"象形字，六画，见 30 页。"虫"作形旁的字多和爬虫有关。虫字旁一般在左侧。

"虫" is a 6 stroke pictogram (see p. 30). The pictophongrams composed of the signific "虫" relate to insects and reptiles. It's on the left side.

| 蛇 | shé | snake | 毒蛇 dúshé viper |
| | | | 蛇肉 shéròu serpent meat |
| | | | 蛇形 shéxíng snakelike |

| 蛇 | | | | | | | | | |
|---|---|---|---|---|---|---|---|---|---|

| 蜂 | fēng | wasp, bee | 蜜蜂 mìfēng honeybee |
| | | | 蜂蜜 fēngmì honey |
| | | | 马蜂 mǎfēng hornet |

| 蜂 | | | | | | | | | |
|---|---|---|---|---|---|---|---|---|---|

| 虾 | xiā | shrimp | 对虾 duìxiā prawn |
| | | | 虾仁 xiārén shrimp meat |
| | | | 虾米 xiāmǐ dried shrimp |

| 虾 | | | | | | | | | |
|---|---|---|---|---|---|---|---|---|---|

# 【竹部】

"竹"象形字,六画,见 36 页。"竹"作形旁的字多和竹子有关。竹字旁在字的上部,写法有点变形。

"竹" is a 6 stroke pictogram (see p. 36). The pictophongrams composed of the signific "竹" relate to bamboo. When placed on the top, the element "竹" is out of shape a little.

| 简 | jiǎn | simple | 竹简 zhújiǎn | bamboo slip |
| | | | 简单 jiǎndān | simple |
| | | | 简便 jiǎnbiàn | handy |

| 简 | | | | | | | | | |
|---|---|---|---|---|---|---|---|---|---|

| 篇 | piān | a piece of writing | 篇章 piānzhāng | chapters |
| | | | 篇目 piānmù | table of contents |
| | | | 篇幅 piānfu | length (of writing) |

| 篇 | | | | | | | | | |
|---|---|---|---|---|---|---|---|---|---|

| 算 | suàn | calculate | 算盘 suànpán | abacus |
| | | | 计算 jìsuàn | calculate |
| | | | 打算 dǎsuàn | plan |

| 算 | | | | | | | | | |
|---|---|---|---|---|---|---|---|---|---|

| 答 | dá | answer | 回答 huídá | answer |
| | | | 答复 dáfù | answer |
| | | | 答谢 dáxiè | express appreciation |

| 答 | | | | | | | | | |
|---|---|---|---|---|---|---|---|---|---|

| 等 | děng | class, equal, wait | 等级 děngjí | grade |
| | | | 相等 xiāngděng | equal |
| | | | 等候 děnghòu | wait |

| 等 | | | | | | | | | |
|---|---|---|---|---|---|---|---|---|---|

| 笑 | xiào | smile | 笑容 xiàoróng | smiling expression |
| | | | 微笑 wēixiào | smile |
| | | | 笑话 xiàohuà | joke |

| 笑 | | | | | | | | | |
|---|---|---|---|---|---|---|---|---|---|

# 【舟部】

象形字,六画,见 39 页。"舟"作形旁的字多和船有关。舟字旁一般在字的左侧。

"舟" is a 6 stroke pictogram (see p.39). The pictophongrams composed of the significant "舟" relate to boat and ship. It's on the left side.

## 船

chuán    boat, ship

| 轮船 | lúnchuán | steamer |
| 船员 | chuányuán | ship's crew |
| 船只 | chuánzhī | shipping |

| 船 | | | | | | | | | |
|---|---|---|---|---|---|---|---|---|---|

## 航

háng    boat, navigate

| 航行 | hángxíng | navigate by water |
| 民航 | mínháng | civil aviation |
| 航海 | hánghǎi | navigation |

| 航 | | | | | | | | | |
|---|---|---|---|---|---|---|---|---|---|

## 般

bān    sort, kind

| 一般 | yībān | general |
| 这般 | zhèbān | such |
| 般配 | bānpèi | suitable |

| 般 | | | | | | | | | |
|---|---|---|---|---|---|---|---|---|---|

# 【衣部】

"衣"象形字,六画,见 42 页。"衣"字作形旁的字大多和衣服有关。衣字旁在左侧时写作"衤"。

"衣" is a 6 stroke pictogram (see p.42). The pictophongrams composed of the significant "衣" relate to clothes. When placed on the left side, "衣" is written as "衤".

## 装

zhuāng    clothing, load

| 服装 | fúzhuāng | clothing |
| 装扮 | zhuāngbàn | dress up |
| 装备 | zhuāngbèi | equip |

| 装 | | | | | | | | | |
|---|---|---|---|---|---|---|---|---|---|

## 衬

chèn    line, lining

| 衬衫 | chènshān | shirt |
| 衬衣 | chènyī | underclothes |
| 衬托 | chèntuō | set off |

| 衬 | | | | | | | | | |
|---|---|---|---|---|---|---|---|---|---|

183

被　　bèi　　quilt

| 被子 | bèizi | quilt |
| 被褥 | bèirù | bedding |
| 被迫 | bèipò | be compelled |

| 被 | | | | | | | | | | | |

## 【米部】

"米"象形字,六画,见19页。"米"作形旁的字多和粮食有关。米字旁多在左侧。
"米" is a 6 stroke pictogram (see p.19). The pictophongrams composed of the signific "米" relate to rice and grain. It's on the left side.

糠　　kāng　　chaff, bran

| 米糠 | mīkāng | rice bran |
| 谷糠 | gǔkāng | husk |
| 糠醛 | kāngquán | furfural |

| 糠 | | | | | | | | | | | |

糖　　táng　　sugar

| 白糖 | báitáng | refined sugar |
| 红糖 | hóngtáng | brown sugar |
| 糖果 | tángguǒ | sweets |

| 糖 | | | | | | | | | | | |

粗　　cū　　coarse, wide, thick

| 粗细 | cūxì | thickness |
| 粗心 | cūxīn | careless |
| 粗暴 | cūbào | rude |

| 粗 | | | | | | | | | | | |

## 【走部】

"走"会意字,七画,见84页。"走"作形旁的字多和走的动作有关。走字旁一般在字的左侧。
"走" is a 7 stroke associative character (see p.84). The pictophongrams composed of the signific "走" relate to walking. It's on the left side.

越　　yuè　　get over, jump over

| 越过 | yuèguò | cross |
| 越野 | yuèyě | cross-country |
| 超越 | chāoyuè | surmount |

| 越 | | | | | | | | | | | |

| 赶 | gǎn | catch up with | 赶快 gǎnkuài | quickly |
| | | | 赶忙 gǎnmáng | hurry |
| | | | 赶上 gǎnshàng | overtake |

| 赶 | | | | | | | | | | | |
|---|---|---|---|---|---|---|---|---|---|---|---|

| 起 | qǐ | stand up | 起来 qǐlái | stand up |
| | | | 起床 qǐchuáng | get up |
| | | | 起动 qǐdòng | start |

| 起 | | | | | | | | | | | |
|---|---|---|---|---|---|---|---|---|---|---|---|

# 【足部】

"足"象形字,七画,见 43 页。"足"作形旁的字多和脚的动作有关。足字旁在左侧时写法有点变形。

"足" is a 6 stroke pictogram,（see p. 43）. The pictophongrams composed of the signific "足" relate to the movement of foot. When placed on the left side, "足" is written as " ".

| 跳 | tiào | jump, leap | 跳高 tiàogāo | high jump |
| | | | 跳远 tiàoyuǎn | long jump |
| | | | 跳舞 tiàowǔ | dance |

| 跳 | | | | | | | | | | | |
|---|---|---|---|---|---|---|---|---|---|---|---|

| 路 | lù | road, way | 马路 mǎlù | road |
| | | | 道路 dàolù | road |
| | | | 走路 zǒulù | walk |

| 路 | | | | | | | | | | | |
|---|---|---|---|---|---|---|---|---|---|---|---|

| 跟 | gēn | heel, follow, with | 脚跟 jiǎogēn | heel |
| | | | 跟着 gēnzhe | follow in the wake of |
| | | | 跟随 gēnsuí | follow |

| 跟 | | | | | | | | | | | |
|---|---|---|---|---|---|---|---|---|---|---|---|

| 踢 | tī | kick | 踢球 tīqiú | kick a ball |
| | | | 踢开 tīkāi | kick away |
| | | | 踢翻 tīfān | kick over |

| 踢 | | | | | | | | | | | |
|---|---|---|---|---|---|---|---|---|---|---|---|

# 【言部】

"言"指示字，七画，见54页。"言"作形旁的字多和说话有关。言字旁在左侧时写作"讠"。

"言" is a 7 stroke indicative character (see p.54). The pictophongrams composed of the signific "言" relate to speaking. When placed on the left side, "言" is written as "讠".

说　shuō　speak, talk, say

| 说话 | shuōhuà | speak |
|------|---------|-------|
| 说明 | shuōmíng | explain |
| 听说 | tīngshuō | be told |

| 说 | | | | | | | |
|---|---|---|---|---|---|---|---|

话　huà　word

| 说话 | shuōhuà | speak |
|------|---------|-------|
| 谈话 | tánhuà | talk |
| 讲话 | jiǎnghuà | speak |

| 话 | | | | | | | |
|---|---|---|---|---|---|---|---|

语　yǔ　language

| 语言 | yǔyán | language |
|------|-------|----------|
| 语法 | yǔfǎ | grammar |
| 汉语 | Hànyǔ | the Chinese language |

| 语 | | | | | | | |
|---|---|---|---|---|---|---|---|

谢　xiè　thank

| 谢谢 | xièxie | thanks |
|------|--------|--------|
| 感谢 | gǎnxiè | thanks |
| 谢意 | xièyì | gratitude |

| 谢 | | | | | | | |
|---|---|---|---|---|---|---|---|

谈　tán　talk, chat, discuss

| 谈话 | tánhuà | conversation |
|------|--------|--------------|
| 谈论 | tánlùn | discuss |
| 商谈 | shāngtán | negotiate |

| 谈 | | | | | | | |
|---|---|---|---|---|---|---|---|

课　kè　course, class

| 上课 | shàngkè | go to class |
|------|---------|-------------|
| 课本 | kèběn | textbook |
| 课程 | kèchéng | course |

| 课 | | | | | | | |
|---|---|---|---|---|---|---|---|

| 请 | qǐng | request, invite | 请客 qǐngkè | stand treat |
| | | | 请问 qǐngwèn | excuse me |
| | | | 请教 qǐngjiào | ask for advice |

| 请 | | | | | | | | | |
|---|---|---|---|---|---|---|---|---|---|
| | | | | | | | | | |

| 读 | dú | read | 读书 dúshū | read |
| | | | 朗读 lǎngdú | read aloud |
| | | | 读者 dúzhě | reader |

| 读 | | | | | | | | | |
|---|---|---|---|---|---|---|---|---|---|
| | | | | | | | | | |

| 谁 | shuí | who | 谁的 shuíde | whose |
| | shéi | | 谁说 shuíshōu | who speak |
| | | | 谁去 shuíqù | who go |

| 谁 | | | | | | | | | |
|---|---|---|---|---|---|---|---|---|---|
| | | | | | | | | | |

| 认 | rèn | recognize | 认识 rènshi | know |
| | | | 认为 rènwéi | consider |
| | | | 认真 rènzhēn | conscientious |

| 认 | | | | | | | | | |
|---|---|---|---|---|---|---|---|---|---|
| | | | | | | | | | |

| 让 | ràng | give way, let | 让步 ràngbù | make a concession |
| | | | 谦让 qiānràng | modestly decline |
| | | | 让座 ràngzuò | offer one's seat to sb. |

| 让 | | | | | | | | | |
|---|---|---|---|---|---|---|---|---|---|
| | | | | | | | | | |

# 【雨部】

"雨"象形字,八画,见44页。"雨"作形旁的字多和云雨现象有关。雨字旁多在字的上部。

"雨" is a 8 stroke pictogram (see p.44). The pictophongrams composed of the signific "雨" refer to meteorological phenomena. It's placed on the top.

| 雪 | xuě | snow | 下雪 xiàxuě | to snow |
| | | | 雪白 xuěbái | snow-white |
| | | | 雪花 xuěhuā | snowflake |

| 雪 | | | | | | | | | |
|---|---|---|---|---|---|---|---|---|---|
| | | | | | | | | | |

雷    léi    thunder

打雷 dǎ léi   thunder
雷声 léishēng   thunderclap
雷鸣 léimíng   thunderous

| 雷 | | | | | | | | | |
|---|---|---|---|---|---|---|---|---|---|

雹    báo    hail

雹子 báozi   hail
冰雹 bīngbáo   hail, hailstone
雹灾 báozāi   disaster caused by hail

| 雹 | | | | | | | | | |
|---|---|---|---|---|---|---|---|---|---|

# 【金部】

"金",八画。"金"作形旁的字多和金属有关。金字旁在字左侧时写作"钅"。

"金" means gold. It has 8 stroke. The pictophongrams composed of the significant "金" relate to metals. When placed on the left side, "金" is written as "钅".

鉴    jiàn    mirror, reflect

鉴别 jiànbié   distinguish
鉴赏 jiànshǎn   appreciate
借鉴 jièjiàn   use for reference

| 鉴 | | | | | | | | | |
|---|---|---|---|---|---|---|---|---|---|

铁    tiě    iron

铁路 tiělù   railway
铁道 tiědào   railway
铁矿 tiěkuàng   iron ore

| 铁 | | | | | | | | | |
|---|---|---|---|---|---|---|---|---|---|

钟    zhōng    bell, clock

钟表 zhōngbiǎo   clocks and watches
钟头 zhōngtóu   hour
分钟 fēnzhōng   minute

| 钟 | | | | | | | | | |
|---|---|---|---|---|---|---|---|---|---|

钱    qián    copper coin, money

钱币 qiánbì   coin
挣钱 zhèngqián   make money
钱包 qiánbāo   wallet

| 钱 | | | | | | | | | |
|---|---|---|---|---|---|---|---|---|---|

镜　　jìng　　mirror

镜子 jìngzi　mirror
眼镜 yǎnjìng　glasses
墨镜 mòjìng　sunglasses

| 镜 | | | | | | | | |
|---|---|---|---|---|---|---|---|---|

## 【食部】

"食"会意字,九画,见 46 页。"食"作形旁的字多和饮食有关。食字旁在左侧时写作"饣"。
"食" is a 9 stroke pictogram (see p. 46). The pictophongrams composed of the signific "食" relate to food. When placed on the left side, "食" is written as " 饣".

餐　　cān　　eat, food

餐厅 cāntīng　dining room
中餐 zhōngcān　Chinese food
西餐 xīcān　Western food

| 餐 | | | | | | | | |
|---|---|---|---|---|---|---|---|---|

饿　　è　　hungry

饥饿 jī'è　hunger
挨饿 āi'è　go hungry
饿殍 èpiǎo　bodies of the starved

| 饿 | | | | | | | | |
|---|---|---|---|---|---|---|---|---|

饱　　bǎo　　be full

吃饱 chībǎo　eat one's fill
饱满 bǎomǎn　full
饱和 bǎohé　saturation

| 饱 | | | | | | | | |
|---|---|---|---|---|---|---|---|---|

馆　　guǎn　　lodging, shop

饭馆 fànguǎn　restaurant
旅馆 lǚguǎn　hotel
茶馆 cháguǎn　teahouse

| 馆 | | | | | | | | |
|---|---|---|---|---|---|---|---|---|

饺　　jiǎo　　dumpling

饺子 jiǎozi　dumpling
水饺 shuǐjiǎo　dumpling
蒸饺 zhēngjiǎo　steamed dumpling

| 饺 | | | | | | | | |
|---|---|---|---|---|---|---|---|---|

# 汉 字 目 录
## CATALOGUE OF CHINESE CHARACTERS

部首和汉字

191

# 音序索引

INDEX OF SYLLABLES OF THE PHONETIC TRANSCRIPTIONS

# 汉 字 字 体

## TYPEFACES OF CHINESE CHARACTERS

| 字体名称<br>Scripts names | 例　字<br>Examples | |
|---|---|---|
| 甲骨文<br>Inscriptions Oracle-Bone | | |
| 篆体<br>Seal Character | | |
| 隶书<br>Official Script | | |
| 楷体<br>Regular Script | | |
| 宋体<br>Song Typeface | | |
| 行书<br>Running Hand | | |
| 草书<br>Cursive Hand | | |